WORDPLAY

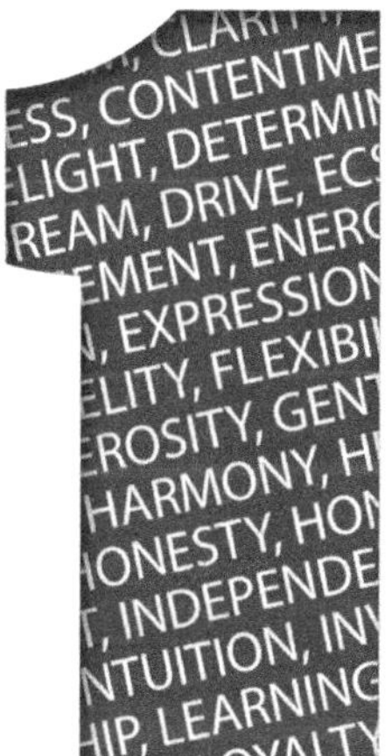
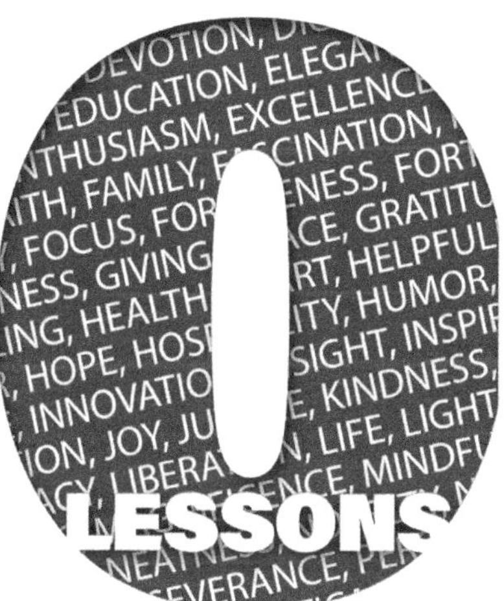

10 LESSONS TO BECOME A BETTER WRITER

DASHAWN TAYLOR

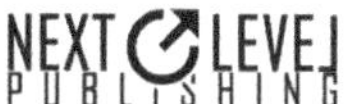

Wordplay: 10 Lessons To Become A Better Writer
ISBN: 978-0-9800154-4-7

NEXT LEVEL
PUBLISHING

For publishing and media inquiries please visit
www.NextLevelPublishng.com or send correspondents to:
Next Level Publishing
14625 Baltimore Ave
#481
Laurel, MD 20707

DEDICATION

★★★

To all the creators out there, who have been gifted with the ability to share their talents with the world, remember this: while the material possessions we accumulate throughout our lives will inevitably pass on to others after we're gone, the impact we make through our actions and contributions can never be taken away.

TABLE OF CONTENTS

INTRODUCTION

It was a typical Tuesday night for bestselling author, Rebecca Roughdraft, as she sat at her wooden desk, surrounded by stacks of paper and books. She was fully immersed in her latest novel, her fingers flying across the keyboard as she brought her characters to life. But suddenly, the room began to shake violently. At first, Rebecca thought it was her imagination, but the shaking grew stronger and more intense with each passing second.

Rebecca stumbled out of her chair and tried to regain her balance as the room shook too violently. She instinctively grabbed her laptop and stumbled towards the door, attempting to escape the chaos. However, the ground beneath her feet was unstable. She heard a deafening roar that seemed to shake the building's foundation.

With dread, Rebecca realized that it was an earthquake. But this was no ordinary tremor. As she made her way out of her apartment, she kept a tight grip on her open laptop. When she reached the street, she was confronted with a scene straight out of a science fiction movie: giant alien creatures had descended upon her housing complex, destroying everything in their path.

The extraterrestrial beings were towering behemoths, standing over three hundred meters tall and making the Empire State Building look like a townhouse. Their massive bodies were covered in dark, scaly armor that glinted menacingly in the sunlight. Their large heads were crowned with jagged spines that jutted out in all directions, and their eyes struck fear into the hearts of everyone running for their lives: they were glowing red orbs that blazed with malevolent energy.

Rebecca looked around in shock and disbelief, witnessing destruction and chaos everywhere. Buildings were collapsing, cars were exploding, and people were running for their lives. The ground was shaking so violently that she could barely stand. She tightened her grip on her laptop and looked for a safe place to run.

As she ran through the streets, dodging debris and fires, she could hear the huge creatures getting closer. Their roars filled the air, making it difficult for her to breathe. But even as the chaos unfolded, Rebecca's mind remained focused on her writing. She found solace in her imagination and continued typing on her laptop, capturing the drama and suspense of the moment in her book.

Rebecca stumbled into a nearby bookstore, seeking shelter from the chaos outside. The shelves were overturned and books were scattered everywhere, but she was undeterred. She found a safe space inside a back room continued writing, her fingers automatically going to the keyboard. The words started to flow, almost as if they were on autopilot. Her writing was a form of escape, a way for her to cope with the terror that surrounded her.

Hours passed, and the shaking finally subsided. Rebecca emerged from the bookstore, her book complete and her spirit unbroken. The city was in ruins, but she was determined to rebuild, both in her writing and in her life. She knew that her book would serve as a testament to the strength of the human spirit, even in the face of the unimaginable.

Of course, the above tale is fictional in nature but relevant in context. There is a Rebecca Roughdraft inside each of us, determined to overcome the obstacles, distractions, and blocks on the path to completing the work that inspires us. We all have the ability to be great communicators through writing. Sometimes we just need to awaken that ability to create a project that could change our lives and the lives of our readers.

The journey to becoming a successful writer is challenging, but it can be incredibly rewarding as well. It requires a combination of creativity, dedication, and a solid understanding of the craft of writing. You should expect to spend long hours sitting in front of a computer, sometimes feeling like you're not making any progress, but also be prepared for moments of pure joy when you finally have a breakthrough in your writing. Despite the challenges, the satisfaction of completing a book or project and sharing your work with readers and fans makes all the hard work worth it.

What makes putting forth written works so special? Well, for starters, it's a way to share your story with the world. Whether you're writing a memoir, a novel, or a guidebook or a piece of literature for digital consumption, your words have the power to touch people's lives and make a difference in the world. It can be an amazing accomplishment.

Writing is also a way to express yourself, to tap into your creativity, and to grow as a person. It's a journey of self-discovery, where you get to explore your thoughts, beliefs, and emotions. And the best part? You get to share those experiences with others, who will learn from your story and be inspired by it. Always remember that your written works have the potential to make a positive impact on the lives of others. Whether you write to educate, inspire, or entertain, you have the opportunity to make a difference in the world through your words.

With over two decades of experience, I have been blessed to share my gift with millions of readers worldwide. My name has been associated with various titles, including Best-Selling Author, New Media Publisher, Executive Producer, Screenwriter, Ghostwriter, and even Speech Writer. My work has appeared in numerous media outlets, such as Time Magazine, MTV, ABC, HBO, VH1, BET, Essence Magazine, and NBC. I have collaborated with world leaders, Oscar-winning actors, NFL Super Bowl champions, Grammy award-winning performers, and dozens of celebrities in various fields. Some of my work has made it onto the New York Times bestseller list, and some have even been adapted for the silver screen.

Throughout my many years in this industry, one constant has always remained. Every project starts with a blinking cursor at the top of a blank white page, ready to be filled with new ideas and creativity.

Stories have a magical way of capturing our hearts and imaginations. They've been passed down from generation to generation, playing a vital role in preserving important lessons, customs, and beliefs. Writing is a craft that requires skill, especially when it comes to connecting with others through words. To be considered a talented writer is a remarkable accomplishment and should be celebrated. And for those who are still in the process of bringing their writing to life, the bravery it takes to share your talent is commendable.

If you've made it this far, it's safe to assume that you're serious about honing your talent and pushing forward to publish an outstanding project. Congratulations! You've taken the first step towards elevating your writing game. "*Wordplay: 10 Lessons to Become A Better Writer*" is the ultimate companion for writers who are serious about sharpening their skills and publishing works that will leave a lasting impact.

In this guide, you'll find a wealth of tips, lessons, and inspiration to help you bring your writing to the next level. I'll cover the art of writing and explore the techniques and habits used by successful writers to turn their ideas into a polished product. Whether you're struggling to find inspiration, feeling unmotivated, or facing writer's block, "Wordplay" will equip you with the tools and encouragement you need to overcome these obstacles and reach the finish line.

You will discover how to create a mental environment that fosters creativity and enables you to write with ease. I will also reveal the (not-so) secret formula that sets great writers apart and helps you add that extra spark to your craft. If you've spent weeks, months, or even years considering the possibility of completing your project, the time has finally come for you to take action and complete your journey from idea to published!

Let's Get Started.

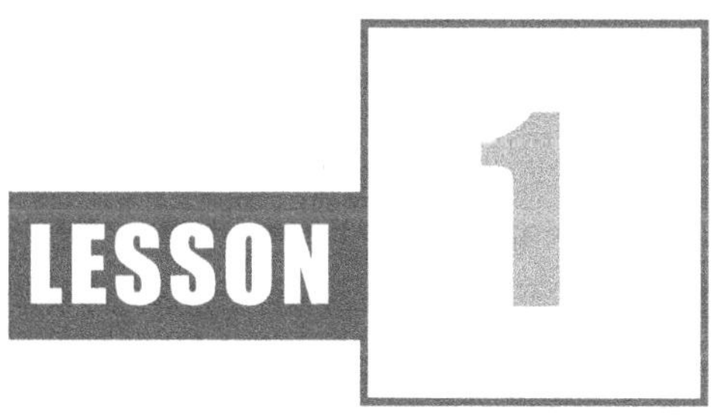

Write What You Love

Tuesday May 26, 2000
8:29pm

I sat silently at my undersized desk, glaring at the 15-inch Dell computer monitor. An intimidating blank white screen stared back at me. I had not written a single word in over two hours. The blank cursor was blinking fast and seemed to be in sync with my racing heartbeat. I was already a full 48 hours behind my deadline. Just two days earlier, my business partner Kyle Newsome and I had purchased our first website domain.

Real-HipHop.com was going to be the next big thing in online music and news. Our dream was to bring the exciting culture of hip-hop to millions of fans across the world through our own digital platform. The vision was getting off to a shaky start. I was having difficulty deciding on the topic for the first article on the website. Was I going to write about how a Detroit rapper named Eminem had just dropped his second album? Or should I write about the secret tip that we received that the Wu-Tang Clan was in the studio working on their third studio album, entitled "The W"? There were so many exciting stories to choose from.

My brain was grappling with the possibilities. As I thought about the hundreds of artists, thousands of songs, and dozens of stories I could choose from, my brain started to fall into what I would later learn was "analysis paralysis." I couldn't make a decision on which way to proceed because I was spending too much time overthinking my strategy. About two hours later, I was still glued to the white screen on my desktop. My business partner Kyle walked into the room and noticed that I had not written a single word. I told him that I was still stuck on which story could make the biggest impact.

Kyle thought for a moment and simply said four words. I remember it clearly, as if it happened yesterday. These four words have stayed with me throughout my career and motivated me to continue crushing projects and reaching heights I never imagined. I ended up writing the words on a small piece of paper and taping it to my monitor. These words guided me every day as Kyle and I produced one of the hottest Hip-Hop websites in the history of the culture. In just three short years, our website reached the elusive goal of one million unique users. The success of our news portal started with these four simple words:

“Write What You Love!”

Writing a book and developing content can be a thrilling and demanding adventure. For those who are enthusiastic about their work, the benefits can be priceless. As a successful author, my advice to aspiring writers or novelists who want to make their impact in the literary world is simple: write what you love.

It is a common misconception that writing a project is simply a matter of putting pen to paper and letting the words flow. In reality, writing is a complex and demanding process that requires a great deal of dedication and hard work. For this reason, it is essential that aspiring writers find their passion and let it guide their writing. This is where the advice “write what you love” comes in.

Best-selling author J.K. Rowling, known for her iconic Harry Potter series, understands the importance of writing what you love. In a recent interview, she stated, “The stories we love best do live in us forever. So, whether you come back by page or by the big screen, Hogwarts will always be there to welcome you home." Her advice to aspiring writers is to find their passion and let it guide their writing. Whether you're writing about magic, mystery, or romance, it is important to have a deep love and connection to your story, as this will shine through in your writing.

Similarly, acclaimed author Stephen King, known for his masterful storytelling, also believes that the key to writing a successful book is to write what you love. He says, "If you don't have the passion for it, it's going to be a chore, and it will show in the final product." King's works are renowned for their depth and emotional impact, and it is clear that his love for writing shines through in every sentence he writes.

For those who are just starting out on their writing journey, it can be helpful to remember that the process of writing a book can be long and challenging. But with perseverance and a love for the craft, the end result can be a piece of work that is both meaningful and fulfilling. The first step is to find your passion, and the rest will follow.

Finding a subject you are passionate about is key to writing a captivating and impactful story. One way to find what you love is to reflect on your interests and hobbies: Think about what you love to do in your free time and what you are knowledgeable about. This could be anything from gardening to hiking to cooking to playing video games. If you are passionate about something, there is a good chance that you could turn that into a story.

Discovering your passion can be as simple as looking into your emotions. What are the things that evoke strong feelings in you? It could be a social cause you care deeply about, a traumatic event, or a significant moment in your life. Writing about these emotional experiences can bring a personal connection between you and the reader, making your writing more authentic and impactful.

When you write from the heart, your writing will be more relatable and your readers will connect with your story. Emotions also play a crucial role in creating vivid characters and scenes in your writing. Consider how the emotions you are exploring can bring your characters to life and create an engaging storyline.

Don't hold back on exploring different emotions in your writing, including negative ones such as fear, anger, and sadness. These challenging emotions can be just as impactful as writing about happiness and joy. The beauty of creativity is that there are no boundaries to what you can express. With an open and imaginative mind, the potential in your writing is limitless. By honing your writing process, you'll be able to tap into the power to bring entire worlds and characters to life. This is when your deeper level of creativity and imagination truly shines through.

Finding a Deeper Level Of Inspiration

First, it's important to understand that your mind is not limited to what you see, hear, and experience in the physical world. The power of the mind extends beyond our world and its experiences. By accessing the universal energies and ideas, one can tap into a wealth of creative inspiration. This technique is commonly practiced by successful authors and is recognized for its ability to enhance creativity and broaden one's capabilities. To fully understand this concept, it is important to recognize the mind's ability to expand beyond its physical limitations and connect with these universal sources of inspiration.

One way to access this creative energy is through meditation and mindfulness practices. By quieting your mind and focusing on the present moment, you can connect with the deep wisdom and creativity that lies within you. This inner wisdom can then be channeled into your writing, helping you to craft more imaginative and captivating stories.

Did you know that each one of us has the power to bring our writing dreams to life? By focusing your thoughts and beliefs on the outcomes and experiences you want to create, you can gain access to a powerful force that can make your writing soar. Always remember to cultivate an open and receptive mindset when it comes to your writing. This means letting go of preconceived notions and limiting beliefs and being open to new ideas and perspectives. By keeping an open mind, you allow yourself to access a wider range of creative ideas and approaches, leading to more innovative and unique stories.

As you procced through your writing journey, think about the impact of energy and vibration on your writing. Everything in the universe, including your thoughts and emotions, has a unique energy frequency. By focusing on positive and creative thoughts and emotions, you can raise your energy frequency and attract more of these experiences and ideas into your life, including your writing. This can lead to a richer, more fulfilling creative experience.

The Power of High Frequency

According to various spiritual and metaphysical beliefs, the emotion that is often considered to have the highest frequency is love. Love is often thought to be the purest and highest vibrational emotion, which has the power to positively impact the frequency of other emotions and thoughts. When we cultivate love, we raise our energy frequency and can attract more positivity, abundance, and creativity into our lives. This is why love is considered to be the highest frequency emotion in many spiritual and metaphysical traditions.

There is no mistake that this lesson is entitled "Write What You Love". It's a challenge for all writers to keep their vibration high during the creative process which will give you the creative fuel to reach the finish line. An effective way to maintain a high frequency level is to focus on your passion. When you write about something you are passionate about, your energy frequency will naturally rise. Your passion will shine through in your writing and your readers will feel your energy and enthusiasm.

A major part of keeping a high frequency when writing is avoiding negative and limiting beliefs. Limiting beliefs and negative thoughts can have a significant impact on a person's life and their ability to achieve their goals and aspirations. These limiting beliefs and negative thoughts can act as a roadblock, preventing a person from moving forward and reaching their full potential. They can create a vicious cycle of self-doubt, fear, and anxiety, which can be difficult to break free from.

It is important to recognize that these limiting beliefs and negative thoughts are just that - thoughts. They are not necessarily a reflection of reality or a person's true abilities. By becoming aware of these limiting beliefs and negative thoughts, a person can then work on releasing them and replacing them with more positive and empowering beliefs. Positive self-talk and affirmations can be a great tool in helping to shift your mindset and maintain a high frequency level. When you repeat positive affirmations to yourself, you are reinforcing the idea that you are worthy and capable of creating great things. This can help you to build confidence, boost your self-esteem, and develop a more positive outlook on life.

Ultimately, it is important to remember that your thoughts and beliefs have the power to shape your reality. By letting go of limiting beliefs and negative thoughts and focusing on positive self-talk and affirmations, you can raise your energy frequency, attract more positive experiences and ideas, and achieve greater success and fulfillment in your journey as an author.

The River of Creativity

When I think of my own writing I try to imagine my creativity as an infinite river. Writing, like a river, is a dynamic and influential force that can inspire countless people. Just as a river has the capability to shape landscapes, provide sustenance, and bring life to its surroundings, writing has the power to evoke emotions, spark new ideas and perspectives, and entertain readers and fans in every corner of the globe.

However, just as a river can be obstructed by elements such as rocks, logs, and dams, our creative energy as writers can also be hindered by obstacles that stand in the way of our progress. These barriers can stifle our motivation, inspiration, and ability to bring our ideas to life, much like a dam that slows down or stops the flow of water. These obstacles can take different forms, such as self-doubt, fear of failure, or feelings of inadequacy. These barriers can be so intense that they leave us feeling stuck and unable to continue. They can be incredibly detrimental to our creative process, just as obstacles in a river can slow down or even stop its flow.

Like a river that gracefully navigates through hindrances and continues to flow, we too can conquer the obstacles in our way. To achieve this, it's vital to tackle these barriers straight on, realizing that they don't reflect our capabilities, but are just thoughts or beliefs that have gradually accumulated in our mind. Engaging in visualization and positive self-talk can help an author navigate around the obstacles and keep the creative river flowing. Changing our negative thoughts to positive ones can unleash our full creative potential, just as removing a dam from a river can allow it to reach its full potential. We can start by altering our negative thoughts, replacing them with positive affirmations and visualization exercises.

For instance, instead of focusing on our weaknesses, we can focus on our strengths and abilities as a writer. We can envision ourselves as successful authors, imagine our writing being celebrated by readers, and constantly remind ourselves of our worth and value as writers. By overcoming the obstacles that hinder our creative energy, we can unleash our full potential as writers and bring our ideas to life.

Inhale deeply and release the obstacles that are holding you back. Visualize your imaginative power as a surging river, irrepressible and mighty. Unleash your thoughts and let inspiration guide you. Who knows what impact and transformation you'll unleash upon the world through your writing!

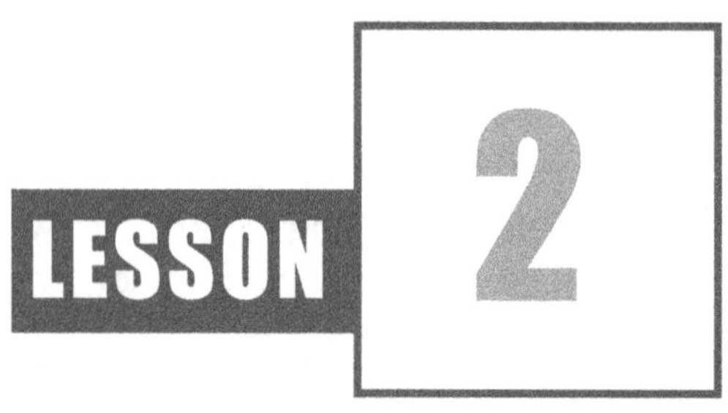

SET GOALS

INT. BRIEFING ROOM - DAY

The room is filled with the low murmur of voices as a group of authors sit at a long wooden table, waiting for the briefing to begin. A large book cover of the target is tacked to the wall at the front of the room.

CAPTAIN TYPEZALOT stands at the head of the table, his arms crossed as he studies the book cover. His eyes are intense, and his jaw is set in determination. The room falls silent as he clears his throat.

CAPTAIN TYPEZALOT:

"Ladies and Gentlemen, we have a tough mission ahead of us. Our target is a highly coveted published book, one that will take our writing careers to the next level. But, the competition is fierce and the publishing industry is highly selective. We need to plan this attack thoroughly and write the best book possible to take down the target."

The authors shift in their seats, exchanging uneasy glances.

CAPTAIN TYPEZALOT:

"But we are talented writers, and we have been preparing for this moment for months. We have the skills, the imagination, and the drive to complete this book and see it published."

The authors nod in agreement, their faces set in determined expressions.

CAPTAIN TYPEZALOT:

"The plan is simple. We'll be breaking into two groups. Group one will focus on researching the market and determining what will make our book stand out. Group two will focus on writing and refining the book until it is ready for publishing."

The room is filled with a low rumble of excitement as the authors begin to discuss the plan and make final preparations.

EXT. WRITING STUDIO - NIGHT

The night is dark, and the only sound is the quiet tapping of keyboard keys as the two groups of authors work tirelessly to complete their book. Group one moves methodically, gathering information and making notes as they determine what will make their book stand out.

Group two moves with purpose, crafting sentences and perfecting their characters until the book is a seamless masterpiece.

INT. PUBLISHING OFFICE - DAY

The authors stand in front of a publisher's desk, their eyes fixed on the manuscript in front of them. CAPTAIN TYPEZALOT reaches out and slides the book toward the publisher.

CAPTAIN TYPEZALOT:

"It's done. We've written the best book possible and now it's time to see if it's good enough to take down the target."

The publisher takes the book, flipping through the pages with a critical eye. Finally, she looks up, a smile spreading across her face.

PUBLISHER:

"Congratulations, this book is exceptional. I'd be honored to publish it."

The authors let out a triumphant shout, their faces alight with excitement and pride.

CAPTAIN TYPEZALOT:

"Ladies and Gentlemen, we did it. We took down the impossible target and proved that we are talented writers.

We may have written a great book, but we'll never forget the sacrifices we made and the hard work we put in to see it published."

The authors nod in agreement, and they turn to leave the publishing office, their heads held high in pride and victory.

FADE TO BLACK

The above screenplay excerpt is a fun illustration of how authors can visualize the process of setting a targeted goal and developing a plan of action to reach the finish line. In the beginning, all projects seem to be an insurmountable task. As a writer, I'm sure you know the feeling all too well. You have a great idea for a book or a project, you've spent hours researching, outlining, and perhaps even writing a few pages. But then, suddenly, you hit a wall. The motivation wanes, the passion fades, and you're left wondering if you'll ever be able to finish what you started.

The good news is, you're not alone. Many writers struggle with completing a project, but there's a simple solution: set specific writing goals. Whether it's writing a certain number of words each day or completing a chapter by a certain date, having clear, achievable goals can help you stay on track and motivated.

The first step in setting specific writing goals is to determine what kind of writer you are. Some writers prefer to write in short bursts, while others prefer to write for longer periods of time. Some writers like to set goals based on word count, while others prefer to focus on the number of pages they complete each day. No matter what your preferred style is, setting a goal that works for you is essential to your success.

Once you've determined what kind of writer you are, it's time to set your goals. A good rule of thumb is to start small and gradually increase your goals as you build momentum. For example, if you're a beginner writer, you might start by setting a goal of writing 500 words per day. As you get more comfortable with your writing, you can gradually increase your goal to 1,000 words per day, or even 2,000 words per day. Set achievable goals. Breaking your writing process down into smaller, achievable goals can help you stay motivated and focused.

Another way to set specific writing goals is to focus on completing a chapter or section by a certain date. This type of goal can be especially helpful for writers who are working on longer projects, as it gives them a sense of progress and helps them stay motivated. For example, you might set a goal to complete a chapter or section by the end of each week. After a number of successful weeks, you can increase your output and set larger goals.

In addition to setting specific writing goals, it's also important to set aside dedicated time for writing. This might mean setting aside an hour or two each day for writing, or dedicating a full day each week to your writing. Whatever works best for you, make sure that you're consistent with your writing time, as this will help you build momentum and stay motivated. Consistency is key when it comes to developing a writing schedule. Try to write every day, even if it's just for a short period of time. This will help you maintain that momentum and make it easier to get into the writing mindset.

Develop A Routine

Human beings are creatures of habit. No matter how much we try to fight it or deny it, at some point in our adult life we will become aware of a vast array of habits and routines that have formed unconsciously due to our past experiences. So, why do we have such a love affair with habits? Is it because they make our lives easier, or sometimes they bring a sense of comfort and familiarity to an otherwise chaotic world? Or is it simply because our brains are wired to crave the routine that habits provide?

The answer is a little bit of everything. You see, habits offer us a predictable routine that can help reduce stress and anxiety. It's like having a trusty map in a foreign land - even if you don't know exactly where you're going, the comfort of knowing you have a plan can make all the difference.

Our brains love habits so much that they've designated a special area just for them - the basal ganglia. This part of the brain is a habit-forming powerhouse, getting stronger and more efficient with each repetition. Before you know it, your habits have taken over and become almost automatic, making it tough to break free.

It's not just our brains that love habits, our emotions do too. Habits provide a sense of comfort and stability in our lives, like a warm blanket on a chilly evening. They offer a predictable routine that we can count on, even on the craziest of days. And when we're feeling overwhelmed, habits can be a lifesaver, giving us a little slice of normalcy in a world that can often feel anything but.

From the beginning of time, habits have played a crucial role in our survival as a species. Our ancestors relied on habits to perform essential tasks like eating and sleeping without having to constantly think about them. This freed up mental space for other critical activities and enabled them to respond promptly to potential dangers. In fact, you could say that our love for habits is wired into us, quite literally!

But habits aren't just limited to the big things in life. No, they can be found in the little moments too. Think about your morning coffee routine, or your bedtime reading ritual. These small habits bring structure and meaning to our daily lives, making us feel more in control and less frazzled. They're like a warm hug in the middle of a busy day, reminding us to slow down and take a moment for ourselves.

So, what can we learn from all this? Well, for starters, that habits are here to stay. They're a big part of who we are as humans, and they play a significant role in shaping our daily lives. But that doesn't mean we can't modify or change our habits. In fact, understanding why we are creatures of habit can be a powerful tool in helping us create new, healthier habits.

Maybe you want to start a daily meditation practice, or maybe you want to break the habit of checking your phone first thing in the morning. Whatever it is, remember that habits take time to form and that change is a slow process. But with a little patience and persistence, you can harness the power of habits to make positive changes in your life and increase your writing productivity.

Schedule Your Success

As a writer, finding the time to write can be a daunting task. Between work, family, and other obligations, it can be difficult to carve out the necessary time to sit down and focus on writing. Your first steps need to include deciding on a time each day that you will dedicate to writing. This might be early in the morning, during your lunch break, or in the evening after dinner. Whatever time you choose, make sure it works for you and that you can commit to it consistently.

A useful strategy to help you stay on track and maintain a clear overview of your writing schedule is to create a visual calendar. You can choose to utilize a whiteboard, a wall planner, or an online tool to map out your writing sessions, which will provide a clear, easily digestible visualization of your workload. Using different colors to highlight various writing tasks such as outlining, drafting, and editing, and incorporating designated time for breaks and relaxation, can help you maintain flexibility while holding yourself accountable. With a visual calendar in place, you can easily track your progress and adjust your schedule as necessary.

When it comes to writing, one of the most significant challenges is maintaining focus and motivation during lengthy writing sessions. It's not uncommon for writers to become distracted or lose focus, resulting in decreased productivity and an increased likelihood of burnout. This is where timers can come in handy.

Timers can be an excellent tool for helping writers stay on track and maintain a flow. By using a timer to break up writing sessions into manageable chunks, writers can improve their ability to focus and reduce the likelihood of fatigue. For example, using a timer to write for twenty-five minutes followed by a five-minute break can help improve concentration and productivity, while also providing a necessary pause to rest and recharge. This option is similar to the Pomodoro Technique, which involves working for twenty-five minutes and then taking a five-minute break, followed by a more extended fifteen to thirty-minute break after four work cycles. This technique can be useful for writers who struggle with maintaining focus and motivation over longer periods.

Breaking up writing sessions into manageable chunks can also help writers maintain momentum and reduce the likelihood of procrastination. By focusing on a specific goal for a limited amount of time, writers can reduce the tendency to become distracted and disengaged. Additionally, by incorporating short breaks into writing sessions, writers can return to the task at hand with renewed energy and motivation.

Another benefit of using timers is that they help writers manage their time more effectively. By setting a specific amount of time for writing, writers can make the most of their available time and ensure they are working towards their goals. This can be especially helpful for writers who have a limited amount of time each day to devote to writing. By breaking up their writing sessions into smaller chunks, they can make the most of their available time and stay on track towards their goals.

Other writers may prefer to use a more flexible timer, such as a digital timer or an app that allows for customized timing intervals. This can be especially useful for writers who work best when they can set their own timing intervals based on their specific needs and preferences.

Adjust Your Schedule When Necessary

Sometimes life happens. Don't beat yourself up about it. As we move through our lives, some things may not go as planned. You may need to adjust your writing schedule to accommodate changes in your routine. Rather than seeing this as a failure, try to see it as an opportunity to be flexible and creative with your updated writing schedule. You can always find time to write, even if it's just for a few minutes at a time. The key is to stay engaged and encouraged, even during challenging stretches.

It's important to remember that writing a book or developing long projects is a marathon, not a sprint. Don't expect to finish in a week or a month. These large endeavors take time and patience, and it's important to be kind to yourself and to celebrate your successes along the way. Whether it's completing a chapter, hitting your word count goal, or simply writing a few pages, take the time to acknowledge your achievements and to stay driven. When you reach a writing goal or milestone, take a moment to acknowledge and celebrate your accomplishment. This will help you stay ambitious and focused on your writing journey.

In conclusion, scheduling writing times and setting writing goals can be challenging, but with the right approach, it's possible to establish a routine and achieve your larger target. By setting specific goals, breaking them down into manageable tasks, holding yourself accountable, being flexible, and celebrating your successes, you can make writing a regular part of your daily routine and achieve the success you deserve.

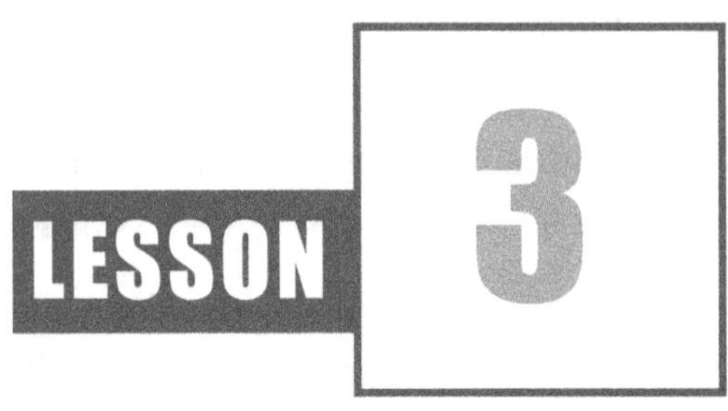

Find Your Voice

> *Feel the rain on your skin, no one else can feel it for you. Only you can let it in, no one else can speak the words on your lips. Drench yourself in words unspoken, live your life with arms wide open. Today is where your book begins, the rest is still unwritten."*
>
> "Unwritten" by Natasha Bedingfield

Wilson A. Bentley lived in the small town of Jericho, Vermont, where he had an insatiable curiosity for the natural world. One cold winter day in the late 1880s, Wilson stumbled upon a discovery that would change the course of his life, and the way we perceive the world around us.

As he walked through his fields, he noticed snowflakes falling from the sky, each one distinct and unique in its shape and pattern. Wilson was amazed by the variation of each snowflake, and saw a connection to the diversity of people on the planet. Determined to capture the beauty of these tiny frozen crystals, he spent years perfecting a method for photographing individual snowflakes. His work showcased the intricacy and uniqueness of each snowflake, and its contribution to the beauty around us.

Just as no two snowflakes are the same, each individual on this planet is unique and contributes to the diversity and vibrancy of our world. The journey of Wilson serves as a friendly reminder that even seemingly ordinary things can have a significant impact, and that by embracing our distinct qualities, we can make a positive difference in the world. Despite facing numerous challenges and obstacles, Wilson remained committed to his passion and persevered through adversity, setting a powerful example for all of us. His work celebrates the beauty of our existence and highlights the extraordinary achievements that can be realized through dedicated pursuit of our dreams.

Just like the billions of snowflakes that cover the ground during winter, each person on our planet is unique and has their own story and perspective. Even if we may share some physical features and behaviors, we all have a distinct experience that sets us apart. Each of us has a different journey, voice, and story to tell when you take a closer look at the human experience.

What Makes Us Different?

When it comes to understanding the human mind, it's easy to fall into the trap of assuming that everyone sees the world in the same way. After all, we all have the same basic sensory equipment, right? But as any experienced psychologist can tell you, the reality is much more complicated than that. As the Rashomon effect illustrates, each of us experiences the world in a unique way, thanks to a complex interplay of factors that range from our individual biology to our past experiences and cultural backgrounds.

The Rashomon effect takes its name from a classic film directed by Akira Kurosawa, in which four witnesses to a crime offer wildly different accounts of what happened. Each witness is convinced that their version of events is the "truth," but the reality is much more elusive. As it turns out, the Rashomon effect is far from fictional - studies have shown that people often interpret the same events in radically different ways, depending on a host of factors.

One such study was conducted by psychologist and philosopher William James back in 1890. James showed participants a drawing of a rabbit, and asked them to describe it. The results were fascinating: while everyone agreed that the drawing depicted a rabbit, their descriptions of the creature varied wildly. Some people focused on its long ears, while others fixated on its short tail or its furry body. Even more strikingly, some participants drew the rabbit facing left, while others drew it facing right.

This early study laid the groundwork for a host of subsequent research into the variability of human perception. In one famous study conducted by psychologists Ulric Neisser and Edward E. Jones in the 1970s, participants watched a video of a woman asking for a donation. Half of the participants were told that she was collecting money for a religious charity, while the other half were told that she was collecting money for a student group. When asked to describe the woman's behavior, participants who believed she was collecting for the religious charity described her as sincere and friendly, while those who believed she was collecting for the student group described her as aggressive and pushy.

These studies illustrate a crucial point: the way we perceive the world is not only influenced by our biology, but also by our past experiences, cultural background, and social context. When we encounter a situation, we draw on a vast array of memories and associations in order to make sense of what's happening. But because these memories and associations are unique to each of us, our interpretations of the situation can be radically different.

So what does this mean for our understanding of the human mind and how we can use it to better our writing and find our voice? For one thing, it suggests that the idea of an "objective" reality is something of an illusion. While we all live in the same physical world, the reality we experience is shaped by the complex interplay of our individual perceptions and interpretations.

As writers, it's easy to fall into the trap of trying to emulate others or follow a set formula for success. But the reality is that each of us brings a unique set of experiences, perspectives, and cultural backgrounds to the writing process. By embracing the Rashomon effect and recognizing that there are countless ways to see the world, we can begin to tap into our own individuality and find our own voice.

Trust Your Instincts

Trusting your instincts is a crucial component of the creative process. As a writer, you bring a unique set of experiences, thoughts, and emotions to your work - and those elements are what make your writing distinct and compelling. By trusting your instincts, you allow yourself the freedom to tap into those experiences and emotions and explore them in your writing.

This means that there is no "right" or "wrong" way to approach a topic when it comes to writing. While there may be certain conventions or guidelines to follow in terms of grammar or structure, the actual content of your writing should reflect your own vision and instincts. Rather than trying to fit your writing into a predetermined mold, you should feel free to explore your own unique perspective on a topic.

For example, if you are writing a piece about a particular social issue, you may have a different viewpoint than other writers. Trusting your instincts in this case means that you should explore your own thoughts and feelings about the issue, rather than trying to conform to what others have written before. By staying true to your own vision and instincts, you may be able to offer a fresh take on the topic that resonates with your readers.

In short, trusting your instincts in your writing means being confident in your own voice and perspective. Rather than worrying about what others may think or trying to conform to a certain style or approach, you should allow yourself the freedom to explore your own unique perspective and bring it to life in your writing. By doing so, you will be able to create something that is truly unique, compelling, and authentic.

Experiment With Different Styles

If you find yourself writing like a robot stuck on repeat, it's time to mix things up and experiment with different writing styles. Think of writing like trying on different hats. Some hats may not be quite right, but others will make you feel like a superstar. Similarly, trying out different styles of writing may not all work for you, but some may feel like a natural fit. One way to experiment with style is to play around with different structures. Instead of sticking to the same old formula, try out new approaches. You could write in short, punchy sentences or long, flowing paragraphs. You could also try out different narrative structures, like non-linear timelines or multiple perspectives. You could play around with writing from different perspectives, like in first-person or third-person point of view. You can also try out different tones and speeds to set the mood of your writing. Whether you want to add some humor or take a more serious approach, the key is to find a style that feels authentic. You could experiment with writing in a more formal or informal style, depending on the audience or purpose of your writing. You could also try incorporating different literary devices, such as metaphors, alliteration, or onomatopoeia, into your writing. The ultimate goal is to find and create a voice for you.

Your Mental Environment

> "*The brain is the hardware, the mind is the software.*"
>
> - Bill Gates

As a writer, your most important asset is your mind. All the research and motivation in the world won't substitute for the importance of having your mind in the right space to create. If I ask you to take a mental picture of your mind, what would you think of? Most people would imagine a snapshot of their brain. This is a reasonable interpretation since the brain is the organ responsible for generating and processing our thoughts and experiences. As a creative person, I can tell you that my level of production and artistic output increased once I started embracing the separation of the brain and the mind.

In a world where success is king and mental agility is a must-have, the brain and the mind have never been more important to writers, authors and content creators. When it comes to achieving your goals and making your mark in the world, understanding the difference between the two is key.

The brain is the hardware of the body - it controls all your physical functions, from moving to breathing to feeling emotions. But the mind is the real star of the show - it's what sets us apart from other animals and more importantly, it's a major part of what separates humans as well. To tap into the power of your mind, it's essential to keep your mental space active, engaged and firing on all cylinders. And when you couple that with a growth mindset (the belief that you can develop and improve through hard work and perseverance), you'll become unstoppable.

The textbook definition of the mental environment refers to the conditions and factors that influence your mental state, such as your thoughts, emotions, beliefs, attitudes, and perceptions. It can be shaped by a variety of internal and external factors, including your personal experiences, social interactions, cultural background, physical health, and environmental factors.

To better enhance and elevate their mental environment, some writers and authors envision their mind as a playground or vast garden that they can cultivate with creativity. Others envision their mind as a bustling city in which to build various locations and domiciles to work in. While still, others view their mental environment as a blank canvas to splatter various colors of artistic expression to pour out to the world. Regardless of which creative metaphor you can develop for your mind, keeping your environment clear and focused will help you expand your mastery of the art.

When searching for your voice, the best place to start is in your mental environment. Because we are all unique individuals, it is very possible that the jewel that you are searching for is hidden in plain sight in your mind's eye. A positive mental environment is one where you feel relaxed, open-minded, inspired, and non-judgmental. This type of mental environment allows for more free-flowing and unconstrained thinking and creativity, which is often crucial for the exploration of unlimited possibilities.

A positive mental environment can also give rise to a sense of curiosity, which is essential to finding your voice. Curiosity is a powerful driving force for creativity because it sparks the imagination and motivates you to explore new ideas and perspectives. By maintaining a sense of wonder and interest in the world, you can find inspiration in everyday experiences and use it to discover and develop your voice. It's important to expand your horizons and break out of your comfort zone. You must stay open to exploring new perspectives, cultures, and ways of thinking. This can lead to a richer, more diverse range of ideas and experiences to draw upon as you develop your voice.

On the flip side, a negative mental environment can actually work against you and be counterproductive to your goals. When you're feeling stressed or overwhelmed, it can be tough to make progress and achieve what you set out to do. It's important to be aware of your mental state and take steps to improve it when needed, so that you can stay on track and reach your full potential.

Writing is a journey of self-discovery. The more you write, the more you will learn about yourself and your writing style. You will find your voice, and it will be unlike anyone else's. Embrace your authenticity and write from a place of passion and purpose.

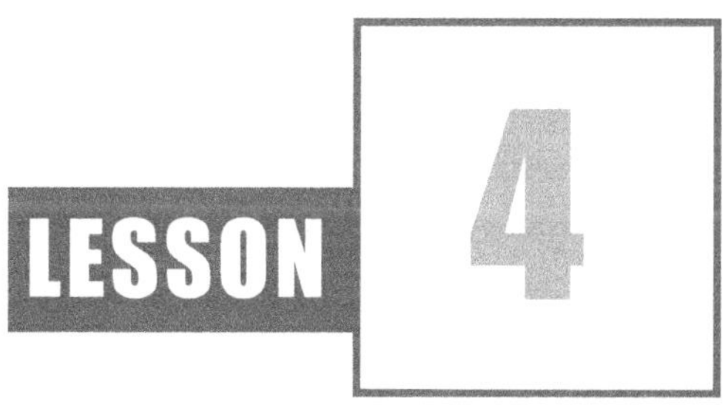

Show, Don't Tell

With your keyboard resting on the desk and a blank computer screen in front of you, you hold the power to create something truly amazing. As a writer, you are the master of your own universe, able to breathe life into characters and spin tales that captivate and inspire. But, as any seasoned writer will tell you, the path to greatness is a winding one. It takes skill, discipline, and a willingness to embrace the power of world building.

In the realm of literary arts, "Show, Don't Tell" is the backbone of writing, the foundation upon which great stories are built. At its core, it's a simple concept: instead of telling your readers what is happening, show them. Don't just say that your character is angry, show your character vehemently slamming their fists on the table and turning burgundy in the face. Don't just tell your readers that it's raining, show them the drops crashing into the pavement and the sound of thunder roaring in the distance.

By using some of the techniques outlined in this lesson, you can draw your readers in on a deeper level. They can become active participants in the narrative, rather than passive observers. This creates a stronger emotional connection between the reader and the story, making it more memorable and impactful.

"Show, Don't Tell" is more than just a technique. It's a mindset. It requires you to think about your writing in a different way, to challenge yourself to be more descriptive and imaginative. It means taking risks, trying new things, and pushing the boundaries of your creativity. It's about bringing your story to life in a way that only you can.

Use Sensory Details

As writers, we are constantly striving to create stories that are vivid and immersive. We want our readers to feel like they are there with us, experiencing the same sights, sounds, and smells that we are. But all too often, some writers fall short of this goal. They struggle to find the right words to convey the rich sensory details that will make their stories come alive.

The solution to this problem is to focus on the sensory details of the world around us. By describing what your characters see, hear, touch, taste, and smell, you can create a rich, multi-dimensional world that your readers can step into. Sensory details are what make your writing come alive. They are essential for captivating readers and creating an engaging experience.

What are sensory details, exactly? They are the bits of information that we take in through our senses. They are the smell of freshly baked bread, the sound of a bird chirping, the feel of a cool breeze on a hot day. By incorporating these details into our writing, we can create a world that feels real and immediate, a world that our readers can see, hear, touch, taste, and smell.

Let's take a look at an example from literature to see how sensory details can be used effectively. In Toni Morrison's "*Beloved*," the protagonist, Sethe, remembers a moment from her childhood when she and her mother were picking berries:

> … Sethe fell down into a place full of strawberry icing, bright with the air of the undiluted summer sun. Like their own mother's milk, it flowed and swirled in their bellies, grew solid in their joints, and beat in their throats. They breathed and

> sucked the taste of it and listened to the music that filled the yard."

In this passage, Morrison uses sensory details to convey the richness and vitality of the moment. We can practically taste the sweetness of the strawberries and feel the warmth of the sun. We can sense the joy and freedom that Sethe is experiencing. It's a powerful moment that sticks with us long after we've finished reading.

Of course, using sensory details effectively is not always easy. It requires a careful balance between description and plot, and it can be all too easy to overdo it. But when done well, sensory details can add a level of richness and depth to our writing that can make it truly memorable.

When describing sensory details, be specific. Instead of simply saying that something smells good, describe the exact scent. Is it sweet? Spicy? Floral? By being specific, we engage our readers with the intent to entertain them to the very end.

Make your characters more lifelike by ensuring to use all of the senses. When we think of sensory details, we often focus on what we see and hear. But don't forget about the other senses, such as taste, touch, and smell. The infusion of sensory details into our written work fosters a rich and intricate reading experience. They are a formidable tool for conjuring mood and tone in your writing. The scent of burning leaves, for instance, can kindle a sense of wistfulness and nostalgia, while the sound of rain tapping against a tin roof can kindle a feeling of snugness and ease.

Character Reveals

In writing, characters are the lifeblood of any story. Even if the story is autobiographical in nature, characters are important. A rich, complex character can make or break a narrative. To create such characters, writers often turn to sensory details, which can help reveal a character's personality and worldview through the things they notice and focus on.

A character's sensory experiences can be used to reveal their preferences, attitudes, and emotions. For instance, a character who is highly sensitive to smells might notice the aroma of a particular perfume or food, and their reaction to that smell can reveal their emotional state or history. Perhaps the scent triggers a memory from their past or elicits a physical reaction, such as a smile or a shudder. Similarly, a character who is visually oriented might focus on the way the light falls on a landscape, and their description of the scene can reveal their artistic sensibility or their emotional response to the setting.

By using sensory details to reveal character, you can create a more nuanced and dynamic understanding of their personality. The way a character experiences the world can be a reflection of their beliefs and background, and by exploring these experiences, you can provide readers with a greater understanding of who the character is and what motivates them.

For example, let's say we have a character named Nicole who is walking down a busy city street. As she passes a bakery, the scent of freshly baked bread wafts into her nose, and she pauses to take a deep breath. This sensory detail can reveal several things about Nicole. Firstly, it suggests that she has a heightened sense of smell, which could be due to her profession, background, or personal preferences. Secondly, it implies that she has an appreciation for simple pleasures, such as the smell of fresh bread. Thirdly, it could indicate that she is feeling a sense of nostalgia or longing, as the scent triggers memories or associations with Nicole's past.

Creating Contrast and Tension

Creating contrast and tension in a story is like the salt and caramel of storytelling - seemingly different, but oh so delicious together. It's a very effective strategy to keep your readers engaged and invested in the story. You can infuse this technique in your writing by using sensory details.

For example, consider a character named John, who is a shy, introverted person. One day, he finds himself in the middle of a crowded, noisy street fair. The sensory details of the scene can be used to create a powerful sense of contrast and tension, as John struggles to navigate the chaotic environment. The noise of the fair can be overwhelming, with the sounds of music, shouting, and laughter blending together in a disorienting cacophony. For John, who is particularly sensitive to noise, this can be a jarring and uncomfortable experience. He might feel as though he is being assaulted by the sensory overload of the fair, and struggle to focus on any one thing.

This use of sensory details to create contrast and tension can be a powerful tool for building suspense and keeping readers engaged. By creating a sense of discomfort or unease in the character, the author can also create a sense of urgency and tension in the reader, who is invested in the character's experience.

In addition to creating contrast between different elements, sensory details can also be used to create tension within a single scene. For example, a character might be in a quiet, serene environment, but the sensory details can hint at an underlying tension or danger.

Consider a character named Natasha, who is strolling through a peaceful forest. The rustling of leaves, the chirping of birds, and the smell of pine all create a sense of calm and serenity. However, the writer might use sensory details to hint at a hidden danger lurking just out of sight. Perhaps the sound of twigs snapping in the distance suggests the presence of an unseen predator, or the sudden silence of the forest hints at an imminent threat.

Employing sensory details to evoke tension within a particular scene can be a potent tool in maintaining reader engagement and emotional investment in the story. By instilling a feeling of expectation and disquietude, an adept author can effectively sustain the reader's sense of intrigue, leaving them eagerly anticipating the unfolding of events.

Sensory Details in Dialogue

When it comes to dialogue, the words that characters speak are only part of the story. The tone, inflection, and body language that accompany those words all work together to convey a character's thoughts, feelings, and motivations. By incorporating sensory details into dialogue, you can create a more vivid and engaging conversation that captures the reader's attention and draws them into the story.

One of the most effective ways to use sensory details in dialogue is to have characters describe the physical sensations associated with their emotions. For example, instead of saying "I'm so hungry," a character could say "I can't stop thinking about that hot, steaming pizza with its gooey cheese and crispy crust." This not only makes the dialogue more interesting, but it also helps to establish the character's state of mind and gives the reader a better understanding of what they are going through.

By using sensory details in dialogue, you can also make the scene more enthralling, allowing the reader to fully experience the character's surroundings. For example, if a character is having a conversation in a coffee shop, the author could describe the aroma of freshly brewed coffee or the sound of the barista grinding beans in the background. This not only adds depth to the scene but also adds color to the character in question.

Another way that sensory details can be used to enhance dialogue is by creating contrast between what a character is saying and what they are actually feeling. This can be particularly effective in dramatic scenes, where characters may be trying to hide their true emotions. By using sensory details to convey the character's inner thoughts and feelings, you can create a sense of tension and suspense that keeps the reader on the edge of their seat.

Of course, it's important to use sensory details in dialogue sparingly and strategically. Overusing them can be distracting or even overwhelming, making the dialogue feel contrived or melodramatic. As with any tool in a writer's toolbox, it's important to use sensory details judiciously and with a clear purpose in mind. Whether used to convey emotion, establish setting, or create suspense, sensory details are an essential element of any well-crafted dialogue.

More Showing Less Telling

As a proficient writer, your capacity to capture the intricacies of the world around you is paramount. Your words have the power to bring entire universes to life, and to do so effectively, you must diligently cultivate your powers of observation. The more attentively you focus on the particulars of your environment, the more proficient you become at communicating them to your audience. But this is not a passive process. You must actively seek out opportunities to observe and capture the details of the world around you. You must train your mind to notice the subtle nuances that make the world so fascinating and complex.

One way to do this is through deliberate practice. Take time to sit and observe the physical world around you. Look closely at the way the light falls on a particular object, the way a leaf flutters in the breeze, the way the steam rises from a hot cup of tea. Try to capture these details in writing, using precise and evocative language. Another way to practice observation is by actively seeking out new experiences. Visit a new place, try a new food, or take up a new hobby. By immersing yourself in new environments and experiences, you challenge yourself to see the world in a different way.

Observation is a crucial skill for writers, and it's about more than just paying attention. To truly observe the world around you, you need to cultivate a sense of curiosity and wonder. This means approaching the world with an open mind, allowing yourself to be surprised and delighted by the unexpected details that emerge. By practicing observation, you can gain a deeper appreciation for the depth and complexity of the world, which will enable you to convey its richness more effectively to your readers.

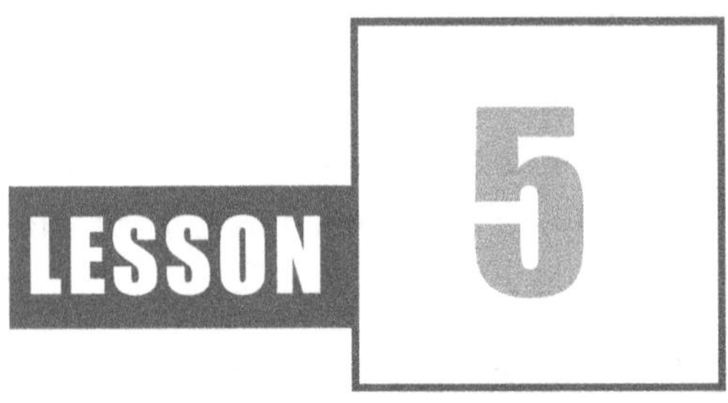

Progress Over Perfection

It is a well-known fact that writers are their own worst critics. Their search for perfection in their work is often never-ending, leading them down a path of constant self-doubt and dissatisfaction. The quest for the perfect book, story or content is a fruitless endeavor, yet many writers cannot help but embark on this journey, hoping to one day achieve literary immortality. In the world of literature, the pursuit for perfection has been a never-ending pursuit. From the aspiring writer who spends years perfecting their manuscript to the seasoned author who obsesses over every sentence, the desire to create the perfect project can be problematic.

The writer's journey is fraught with obstacles, the biggest of which is the notion of perfection. It's the idea that there is a perfect sentence, a perfect story arc, a perfect character. The pursuit of this ideal can be all-consuming, causing writers to obsess over every detail, to the point where they can't move forward with their work.

In reality, perfection is an unattainable goal. It's a myth perpetuated by our society, which values perfection over progress. It's a notion that has been ingrained in us since childhood, where we are taught that anything less than perfect is not good enough. Writers are particularly susceptible to this way of thinking, as their work is often judged on a subjective level. What one reader may find perfect, another may find flawed. And yet, writers continue to strive for perfection, seeking validation from their readers and peers.

But what if we shifted our focus from perfection to progress? What if we saw writing as a journey, rather than a destination? This mindset can be liberating for writers, allowing them to focus on the process of writing, rather than the end result.

The pursuit of perfection is not a new phenomenon in the literary world. In fact, it has been a driving force behind many of the most celebrated works of literature. Writers like Shakespeare, Jane Austen, and Ernest Hemingway all strived for perfection in their writing, and their dedication to the craft has resulted in timeless works that continue to captivate readers today. To be fair, there are many great works of literature were not born out of a quest for perfection, but rather a desire to explore and experiment. Most great writers are known for pushing the boundaries of traditional storytelling, experimenting with language and structure to create works that are groundbreaking for their time. Writing is an art form, and like any art form, it requires skill and craft. But there is a difference between striving for excellence and striving for perfection.

Excellence is a standard that is attainable. It is the practice of honing one's craft, of striving to create work that is polished and refined. Perfection, on the other hand, is a standard that is impossible to achieve. It is an ideal that is constantly out of reach, a carrot on a stick that keeps writers running in circles.

The pursuit of perfection can also lead to a lack of creativity. When writers are too focused on creating the perfect work, they can become paralyzed by the fear of making a mistake. This fear can stifle creativity and prevent writers from taking risks and exploring new ideas.

In contrast, a focus on progress can encourage writers to take risks and experiment with their projects. It allows them to approach their writing with a sense of curiosity and openness, rather than fear and anxiety. Of course, this is easier said than done. The desire for perfection is deeply ingrained in our society, and it can be difficult to overcome. But by recognizing the futility of this pursuit, writers can begin to shift their focus and find greater fulfillment in the writing process.

The notion of a perfect book, story, blog, screenplay, poem or any other literary project is unrealistic. It only exists as an ideal in our minds. Instead of striving for an unattainable goal, writers should prioritize creating work that is true to their voice, authentic, and honest. Crafting work that is genuine and sincere to the writer's voice, not only enhances their fulfillment in their writing, but also improves the probability of establishing a profound connection with their audience.

The journey of a writer is not an easy one, and it is marked by ups and downs, moments of inspiration, and moments of frustration. By embracing the process and letting go of the need for perfection, writers can find greater meaning and purpose in their work. The journey of writing is a journey worth taking, even if it doesn't lead to the destination we originally envisioned.

Work With An Editor

It's a common story: a writer toils away in solitude, perfecting their manuscript until they're convinced it's ready to be published. But when it finally reaches readers, it falls flat. Maybe it's the dialogue that feels forced, or maybe the pacing is off, and the ending is anticlimactic. So where did the writer go wrong?

Often, the answer is that they neglected the crucial step of working with an editor. In today's publishing landscape, it's easier than ever to bypass traditional gatekeepers and put your work out into the world. But the downside of that freedom is that many writers miss out on the invaluable feedback and guidance an editor can provide.

It's understandable why writers might be hesitant to open themselves up to criticism. After all, writing is a deeply personal endeavor. But that doesn't mean it's wise to keep your work in a vacuum. In fact, bringing in a fresh set of eyes can be the difference between a good project and a great one. For one thing, editors have the benefit of distance. While the creator is intimately familiar with the story they're trying to tell, an editor can approach it with fresh eyes and a different perspective. They can point out inconsistencies in character or plot, suggest ways to streamline the narrative, and help the writer clarify their themes.

At the same time, editors are experts in the craft of writing. They can help identify areas where the writer might be relying too heavily on exposition, or where the dialogue is falling flat. They can provide guidance on pacing, structure, and tone. And they can help the writer avoid common pitfalls like clichés, info-dumps, and awkward transitions.

Perhaps most importantly, editors can help writers avoid the trap of perfectionism. Many writers get bogged down in trying to make every sentence and paragraph flawless, to the point where they lose sight of the big picture. An editor can remind them that no book is perfect, and that the goal should be to create a work that is engaging, meaningful, and true to the author's vision.

Of course, not all editors are created equal. It's important for writers to find someone who is not only knowledgeable about the craft, but also someone they trust and respect. Ideally, an editor should be a partner in the creative process, not a dictator who tries to impose their own vision on the writer.

One way to find a good editor is to look for recommendations from other writers or industry professionals. Another is to research editors online, read reviews, and check out their websites and social media profiles. Many editors offer sample edits or consultations, which can be a good way to get a sense of their style and approach. Working with an editor can also be an investment in a writer's career. A polished, professional manuscript is much more likely to attract the attention of agents and publishers, and to stand out in a crowded market. It can also help writers build their skills and confidence, and to develop a thicker skin when it comes to criticism.

Of course, working with an editor is not a magic bullet. It still requires hard work, dedication, and a willingness to be vulnerable. But the rewards can be immense. By collaborating with an editor, writers can hone their craft, improve their work, and ultimately reach more readers. Writing is not a solitary pursuit. It's a conversation between the writer and the reader, and an editor can help ensure that conversation is as engaging, meaningful, and impactful as possible. Working with an editor can be the best decision you ever make to advance your career.

Give Yourself Permission to Make Mistakes

The life of a writer is often romanticized as a solitary and introspective pursuit. But the reality is that writing is a messy, chaotic, and often nerve-wracking experience. Writing requires vulnerability, self-examination, and a willingness to put your innermost thoughts and feelings out into the world for all to see. It can be scary, but it can also be liberating.

One of the biggest hurdles for writers is the fear of making mistakes. We are taught from a young age to strive for perfection, to get it right the first time, and to avoid mistakes at all costs. But the truth is that mistakes are an inevitable part of the creative process, and they can be some of the most valuable learning experiences we have as writers. When we give ourselves permission to make mistakes, we free ourselves from the paralyzing fear of failure. We can experiment, take risks, and try new things without the constant pressure to get it right. And when we inevitably do make mistakes, we can learn from them, grow from them, and use them to become better writers.

Think of it this way: every great writer has made mistakes. Every bestselling novel, every critically acclaimed essay, every Pulitzer Prize-winning play was born out of a process of trial and error. The first draft of anything is rarely perfect, and that's okay. It's only by making mistakes that we can learn what works and what doesn't, and use that knowledge to refine our craft.

Give yourself permission to make mistakes. Embrace them as learning opportunities, rather than failures. Use them to push yourself further and to explore new creative territories. Remember that the writing process is not about getting it right the first time, but about the journey of self-discovery and growth that comes with it. And most importantly, don't be afraid to share your mistakes with others. Share your first drafts, your rough sketches, your half-formed ideas. By being vulnerable and open to feedback, you can learn from others, and grow even more as a writer. Never forget that the most successful writers are not those who have never made a mistake, but those who have learned from their mistakes, grown from them, and used them to become better writers.

Learn When To Let It Go

As writers, we pour our hearts and souls into our work, and it's only natural to want it to be perfect. We revise, edit, and tweak until we feel like we've reached our limit, but sometimes it seems like there's always just one more change we could make. We worry that letting go means admitting defeat, but the truth is that holding onto our work indefinitely only hinders our progress.

Learning to let go is an essential skill for any writer. It's not just about accepting that our work is as good as it's going to get; it's about acknowledging that it's time to move on. When we hold onto a project for too long, we can get stuck in a rut. We might find ourselves making the same changes over and over again, or we might become so attached to our work that we're unwilling to see it in a new light.

So how do we learn to let go? The first step is to recognize that perfection is an illusion. No matter how hard we try, there will always be room for improvement. That's not to say that we should settle for mediocrity, but rather that we should strive for excellence without obsessing over every detail.

The second step is to set a deadline for ourselves. Whether it's a self-imposed deadline or one imposed by a publisher, client or firm, having a concrete goal in mind can help us stay focused and on track. It's important to be realistic about our deadlines, though. Giving ourselves too little time can lead to shoddy work, while giving ourselves too much time can lead to procrastination.

The third step is to seek feedback from others. It can be difficult to assess our own work objectively, so it's helpful to get a fresh perspective. This might mean sharing our work with a writing group, hiring an editor, or simply asking a trusted friend to read it over.

Finally, we need to accept that our work is done when it's done. This doesn't mean that we should stop striving for excellence, but rather that we should recognize when we've reached the point of diminishing returns. It's time to move on to the next project, to continue growing and improving as writers. Letting go can be scary, but it's also liberating. When we stop obsessing over every detail and start trusting our instincts, we can create work that is truly genuine and profound. So let go of your work, and trust that it's the best it can be. Your next project is waiting for you.

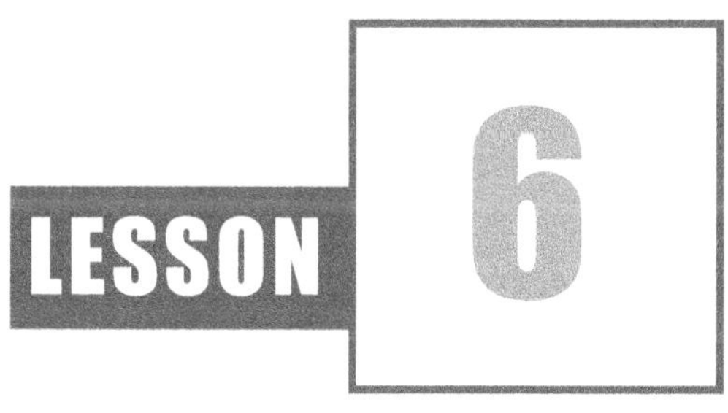

A.R.T.
(Always Remain Teachable)

Anyone who stops learning is old, whether at twenty or eighty. Anyone who keeps learning stays young."

- Henry Ford

Nola Ochs had always loved learning. Even as a child, she would sneak books from her parents' library and read by the light of the moon until she fell asleep. But life had other plans for her. She got married, had four children, and spent most of her adult life running a farm in western Kansas. She never had the chance to finish her education. But in her 80s, Nola started thinking about college again. She had always regretted not finishing, and she realized that she still had a lot to learn. So, she applied to Fort Hays State University, the local college, and was accepted.

At first, Nola was nervous. She hadn't been in a classroom in over 60 years, and she wasn't sure if she would be able to keep up with the younger students. But she soon discovered that she was a natural. She loved the classes, the discussions, and the challenge of learning new things.

Nola's favorite class was history. She had always been fascinated by the past, and now she was able to delve into it more deeply. She would spend hours in the library, poring over old books and documents, trying to piece together the stories of people who had lived centuries before. It wasn't always easy - there were times when she felt swamped, when she doubted herself, when she wondered if she was too old for all of this. But she persevered, and in 2007, at the age of 95, she became the oldest college graduate in history.

Nola's achievement made headlines all over the country. People were inspired by her determination, her passion, and her refusal to let age be a barrier to learning. She was invited to give speeches and interviews, and she became a symbol of the power of education.

But Nola didn't stop there. After she graduated, she continued to teach at Fort Hays State University, inspiring countless students to pursue their dreams, no matter how old they were. And even after she retired from teaching, she remained an advocate for education, traveling around the country to speak to groups of all ages about the importance of lifelong learning.

Nola Ochs may have been the oldest college student ever, but she was also one of the most inspiring. Her love of learning, her passion for history, and her unwavering dedication to education left a legacy that will be remembered for generations to come.

Never Stop Learning

As a writer, it is common to become invested in your own creative process and resist feedback or instruction. Writing is a personal form of expression and can feel like an extension of oneself. However, the benefits of remaining open to learning and guidance can be critical to unlocking your full potential as a writer. Despite your level of experience, continued learning and growth can significantly impact your writing quality. Writing is a craft that can always be refined and improved, and taking a writing class can be an invaluable way to achieve this goal.

Writing classes provide the opportunity for you to receive feedback on your work from experienced instructors and peers. This feedback can help identify your individual strengths and weaknesses as a writer, as well as provide a roadmap for improvement. You can learn new techniques and strategies for creating engaging stories and connecting with your audience.

In addition to the technical benefits of writing classes, they can also help you stay motivated and inspired. Writing can be a solitary and isolating process, but in a classroom setting, you are surrounded by like-minded individuals who share their passion for storytelling. This environment can provide a space for you to connect, share ideas, and establish long-lasting friendships.

For writers looking to take their writing to the next level, or simply connect with a community of writers, taking a writing class is an effective solution. It may spark new creativity and propel you to new heights. Expert authors understand the importance of continuous learning and growth, and being teachable is a vital aspect of a successful writing career.

Join A Writing Community

Writing communities are one of the most essential resources available to any writer. They offer a space for you to connect, collaborate, and share your work, providing valuable feedback and support that can help foster growth and improvement. Joining a writing community can provide many benefits, both practical and emotional. In these communities, you can find like-minded individuals who share your passion for storytelling, and establish meaningful connections with people who understand the challenges and joys of the creative process.

In a writing community, you can also find mentorship and guidance, and gain access to the resources and tools that can help you grow and develop. Whether it's through workshops, classes, or critique groups, you can receive valuable feedback on your work, helping you to identify your strengths and weaknesses and develop your craft. Beyond the practical benefits, writing communities can also provide emotional support for writers. Writing can be a lonely and challenging endeavor, one that requires perseverance and dedication. In a writing community, you can find the motivation and inspiration you need to keep pushing forward, to keep improving and growing, and to stay committed to you craft.

Being part of a writing community requires a willingness to remain teachable and open to feedback, to remain dedicated to the craft, and to be part of a collaborative process that values the contributions of all its members. The rewards of being part of such a community are immeasurable, providing not just the practical tools and resources that writers need to grow, but the emotional support and encouragement that they need to thrive.

Hire A Literary Consultant

A literary consultant is a professional who provides expert guidance and support to writers at all stages of their careers. From aspiring novelists to established writers, a skilled consultant can help creators develop their craft, navigate the publishing industry, and achieve their goals as artists. A consultant can provide feedback and advice on everything from manuscript development to book proposals, query letters, and finding an agent. They can also help writers develop their skills as storytellers, hone their craft, and find their unique voice as artists.

Unlike traditional editors, literary consultants work with writers on a more holistic level, helping them identify and overcome the obstacles that can stand in the way of success. They can offer expert guidance and advice on everything from plot structure and character development to dialogue, pacing, and style. They can also provide a valuable perspective on the business side of writing, helping writers understand the ins and outs of the publishing industry and develop a strategy for success.

One of the primary benefits of working with a literary consultant is the expert guidance and feedback that they can provide. Whether you're just starting out as a writer or you're an established author looking to refine your craft, a consultant can offer valuable insights into what works and what doesn't in your writing. They can help you identify areas for improvement, offer practical advice on how to overcome common writing challenges, and help you develop the skills and knowledge you need to succeed. A literary consultant can also also offer valuable insights into the publishing industry as a whole. They can help you understand how the industry works, what publishers and agents are looking for, and how to position your work in the marketplace. They can also provide valuable connections to agents, producers, filmmakers, publishers, and other industry professionals who can help you advance your career.

A literary consultant can also offer a writer accountability and structure. You can gain valuable assistance with helping you reach your writing goals. They can provide structure and guidance to help you stay on track with your writing, set realistic goals, and measure your progress over time. They can also help you develop a writing routine that works for you, providing practical advice on how to make the most of your time and maximize your productivity.

When selecting a literary consultant, it's important to find someone who is a good match for your personality, style, and goals as a writer. Look for someone who is supportive, encouraging, and who can provide the guidance and feedback you need to succeed. You should feel comfortable discussing your work with your consultant, and should be able to build a relationship based on trust, respect, and open communication.

Experience is key. Look for a consultant who has a proven track record of success, and who has worked with writers at all stages of their careers. A consultant with years of experience in the publishing industry can offer valuable insights and guidance on everything from manuscript development to finding an agent, and can help you navigate the many challenges that come with being a writer. Your literary consultant needs to have a deep understanding of the publishing and entertainment industry. Look for someone who has worked with publishers, agents, and other industry professionals, and who can provide valuable insights into what these professionals are looking for in a manuscript. A consultant with this knowledge can help you position your work effectively, and can provide guidance on how to navigate the industry's many complexities and challenges. It's also important to select a consultant who is available to work with you on a regular basis. Look for someone who has the time and resources to provide the support you need, and who can offer the flexibility and responsiveness required to meet your goals as a writer. A consultant who is overbooked or unavailable may not be able to provide the level of guidance and support you need to succeed.

Be Humble

Writing is a noble pursuit, one that demands nothing less than your very best. It is a craft that requires patience, determination, and a willingness to be both humble and teachable. As writers, we are constantly striving to improve our skills, to find our voices, and to create works that touch the hearts and minds of our readers. To do this, we must remain open to the possibility that there is always more to learn. We must be willing to embrace our status as students of the craft, to remain humble in the face of our successes, and to maintain a growth mindset in all that we do. At the heart of this approach is a deep sense of humility. We must recognize that even the most accomplished writers are always learning and growing, and that there is always more to discover and explore within the world of writing. By remaining humble and teachable, we can unlock the full potential of our creative talents and become truly masterful wordsmiths.

Staying humble and teachable is easier said than done. In a world that often rewards self-promotion and bravado, it can be all too easy to fall into the trap of arrogance and complacency. But as writers, we must remember that our craft demands nothing less than our very best, and that the only way to improve is to remain open to the possibility of growth and knowledge.

In the end, staying humble and teachable as a writer is about more than just improving our skills and finding success in the world of writing. It is about recognizing that writing is a collaborative pursuit, one that requires us to be receptive to feedback, open to new ideas, and willing to learn from others. By embracing this spirit of collaboration and learning, we can become not just better writers, but better human beings, committed to the pursuit of truth, beauty, and excellence in all that we do.

Be Willing to Accept Change

> "*The secret of change is to focus all of your energy, not on fighting the old, but on building the new.*"
>
> – Socrates

We all have a vision for the works we create. It's this vision that we pour our hearts and souls into, and it's this vision that drives us forward in our pursuit of literary excellence. But as the world of writing continues to evolve, it's important that we remain open to change, willing to adapt and change our approach as needed in order to stay current, relevant, and fresh.

The fact is, writing is an ever-evolving field, one that demands that we be constantly aware of new ideas and approaches. In a world where attention spans are growing shorter by the day, and the pace of life is growing faster and more frenetic, writers must find new ways to capture the attention of their readers, to tell their stories in a way that is engaging, relevant, and memorable. To do this, we must be willing to embrace change. We must be open to new ideas, new approaches, and new techniques, always seeking to push the boundaries of what is possible within the world of writing. This means being willing to step out of our comfort zones, to experiment with new styles and genres, and to be bold and daring in our creative pursuits.

Some writers become attached to their comfortable ways of doing things, to their particular styles and techniques. It can be difficult to let go of these things, to step outside of their familiar routines and embrace the unknown. But as the saying goes, change is the only constant in life. If we want to continue to grow and thrive as writers, we must be willing to evolve, to adapt, and to embrace the new and the different. This means being open to feedback from others, seeking out the guidance and mentorship of those who have gone before us, and being willing to take risks and try new things.

Ultimately, staying open to change is about more than just improving our craft as writers. It's about embracing the dynamic, ever-changing nature of the world around us, and finding new ways to connect with our audience and share our stories in a way that is relevant and meaningful. It's about being flexible, adaptable, and resilient, always ready to pivot and shift as needed in order to stay current and on-trend. It's these qualities that will set you apart as a writer, and help you to create works that are cutting-edge, relevant, and trailblazing for years to come.

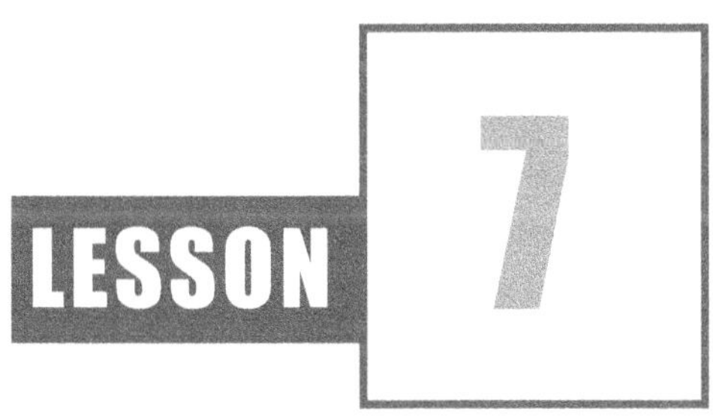

The 3 Rs

(Read, Research, Reflect)

It's often said that great writers are great readers. While this may seem like a simple statement, it's a phenomenon that has been observed time and time again throughout history. From Langston Hughes, to George Orwell to Richard Wright, countless writers have emphasized the importance of reading and how it has influenced their own work. Reading is the foundation of writing. Without it, a writer's work would lack depth, complexity, and creativity. Reading is essential for writers to develop their skills, expand their knowledge, and expose themselves to different perspectives. When a writer reads, they are not only absorbing information but also gaining inspiration for their own work.

For many writers, reading is a form of research. They read books on a particular subject to gain a deeper understanding of it. For example, before writing his novel "The Da Vinci Code," Dan Brown read numerous books on art, history, and religion. By doing so, he was able to incorporate real-life facts into his story, making it more engaging and believable. Learning this fact was especially inspirational to me because before I wrote my first novel "Kissed By The Devil", I actually read "The Da Vinci Code" and also read "The Coldest Winter Ever" by Sister Souljah to find the benchmark to ensure that my debut novel would make an explosion onto the literary scene.

Reading also helps writers to develop their own writing style. By studying other writers, they can learn from their techniques and experiment with their own. For example, Ernest Hemingway was inspired by the simplicity and clarity of the language in the King James Bible, and he incorporated that style into his own writing. In this way, reading can be a form of apprenticeship for writers.

Famous Examples

Ta-Nehisi Coates is a highly regarded American writer and journalist who has been acclaimed for his essays and nonfiction works on race, politics, and culture. Coates grew up in Baltimore, Maryland, and did not have a formal education beyond high school. However, he was a self-taught reader from an early age and was deeply interested in history, politics, and social justice.

Coates has cited a wide range of writers as major influences on his work, including Toni Morrison, James Baldwin, and Richard Wright. Morrison, in particular, has been a significant influence on Coates, who has described her novel "Beloved" as one of the most important books he has ever read. He has also noted the importance of Baldwin's work in shaping his understanding of American society and culture.

In his own writing, Coates has been praised for his ability to engage with complex issues of race and identity in a clear and compelling way. His 2015 book "Between the World and Me," which takes the form of a letter to his teenage son about growing up Black in America, was a critical and commercial success and won the National Book Award for Nonfiction. Coates has also written for a number of publications, including The Atlantic, where he served as a national correspondent, and The New York Times Magazine.

Another famous example is Alice Munro, the celebrated Canadian writer and winner of the Nobel Prize in Literature, is known for her finely crafted and emotionally resonant short stories. Munro has cited a number of writers as major influences on her work, including Anton Chekhov, James Joyce, and William Faulkner.

Munro has spoken of her love of reading, describing it as her "salvation" and a way to escape from the challenges of her own life. She grew up in a small town in Ontario, Canada, and had to navigate personal difficulties, including her father's struggles with mental illness, while also pursuing her own interests and passions.

Despite these challenges, Munro was an avid reader from a young age and devoured a wide range of books and stories. She has described reading as a way to experience new worlds and ideas, to connect with others, and to find comfort and solace in difficult times.

Munro's own writing reflects her deep engagement with the written word, and her stories are marked by a precise attention to detail, a sensitivity to human relationships and emotions, and a commitment to exploring the complexities of everyday life. Her work has been praised for its deep humanity, its honesty, and its ability to capture the nuances of ordinary experience.

Research

As a writer, you may have experienced times when your words don't flow as easily as you would like, or when you feel like you've hit a wall in terms of your development as a creator. This is a common experience, but it doesn't have to be a permanent one. By utilizing research tools and techniques, you can enhance your writing and take your skills to the next level.

One of the primary benefits of research is that it can help you develop a deeper understanding of the subjects you are writing about. Whether you are writing fiction or non-fiction, having a thorough understanding of your topic is critical to making your work compelling and engaging. By conducting research, you can gain insights and information that you may not have been aware of before, which can help you approach your writing with a fresh perspective and incorporate details and nuances that will make your work more authentic and interesting.

In addition to developing a deeper understanding of your subject matter, research can also help you identify gaps in your knowledge. As you dive into your research, you may come across information that you were not previously aware of, or you may discover areas where you need to dig deeper to fully understand a concept or idea. These gaps in your knowledge can be used as a starting point for further exploration and can help you refine your writing and become an expert in your field.

Research can also help you avoid mistakes or inaccuracies in your writing. If you are writing a historical novel, for example, you will need to be accurate in your portrayal of the time period and setting. Research can help you ensure that you are getting the details right, which will make your work more authentic and believable. Similarly, if you are writing about a scientific concept or medical condition, you will need to be accurate in your description of these topics. Research can help you ensure that you are using the correct terminology and accurately representing these concepts, which will make your work more trustworthy and reliable.

Another benefit of research is that it can inspire your writing. By diving deep into your subject matter, you can find new ideas and approaches that you may not have considered before. For example, if you are writing a novel set in ancient Rome, researching the culture and daily life of that time can help you find inspiration for scenes and characters that you may not have otherwise thought of.

So, what are some techniques for utilizing research in your writing? First and foremost, it is important to be strategic in your approach. This means identifying the key questions you want to answer and working systematically to find the information you need. It is also essential to be discerning in your research, evaluating the sources you find and ensuring that they are reliable and trustworthy. In terms of tools and resources, the internet is an invaluable tool for writers. It can be used to access a wide range of information, from scholarly articles to blog posts. In addition to the internet, there are also specialized databases and search engines that can be used to find information on specific topics. Libraries are also a great resource for writers, providing access to books, journals, and other materials that may not be available online.

Once you have gathered your research, it is time to apply it to your writing. There are a number of different ways you can do this, depending on the type of writing you are doing. For non-fiction writing, research can be used to support your arguments and add depth to your analysis. For example, if you are writing an article on climate change, you can use research to provide statistics and data to support your claims.

For fiction writing, research can be used to add detail and texture to your descriptions. For example, if you are writing a novel set in medieval times, researching the clothing, food, and daily life of that period can help you create a rich and vivid world for your readers.

It is also important to remember that research is an ongoing process, and it is important to continue researching even as you are in the middle of your projects. As you write, you may come across new questions or ideas that require further exploration, and it is important to take the time to delve deeper into these topics to ensure that you are presenting the most accurate and compelling information possible.

In addition to being strategic and discerning in your research, it is also important to be ethical. This means properly citing your sources and avoiding plagiarism. Plagiarism is a serious offense in the writing world and can damage your reputation as a writer. By properly citing your sources, you not only protect yourself from accusations of plagiarism, but you also show respect for the work of others and demonstrate your own credibility and expertise.

Finally, it is important to remember that research is just one tool in the writer's toolkit. While research can help you develop a deeper understanding of your subject matter and enhance your writing, it is not the only factor in creating compelling and engaging work. Writing is a craft that requires practice, dedication, and creativity, and it is important to hone these skills in addition to conducting research.

Applying Your Research To Your Work

Research is like a secret weapon for writers - whether you're a grizzled pro or a newbie scribe, it can help you craft stories that are as tantalizing as a juicy steak or as informative as a seasoned tour guide. But like a master chef or a savvy traveler, it's crucial to use your ingredients wisely and strategically, so that your readers are left savoring every last morsel of your words.

When it comes to non-fiction writing, using research to support your arguments and add depth to your analysis can be a powerful tool. This can include using statistics, quotes, and expert opinions to back up your claims and provide evidence for your ideas. However, it is important to use this information in a way that is clear and concise, avoiding overwhelming the reader with too much technical detail. Instead, use your research to provide support for your main ideas and help the reader better understand your perspective.

In fiction writing, research can be used to add detail and texture to your descriptions, creating a more vivid and immersive world for your readers. This can include researching historical events, cultural traditions, or even the natural world to add depth and nuance to your setting, characters, and plot. By using research in this way, you can create a more authentic and believable world for your readers to explore.

As you apply your research to your writing, it is important to do so in a way that feels natural and seamless. It should enhance your writing, not detract from it, and it should be woven into the text in a way that feels organic and purposeful. This can be achieved by carefully selecting the information you want to include, and finding ways to integrate it seamlessly into the overall narrative.

Reflect

Writing is a craft that takes practice and dedication to master. As you work to improve your writing skills, it's essential to not only read and research but also to reflect on your writing process and the work you produce. Reflection allows you to identify areas of strength and weakness in your writing, develop your voice, and continue to grow as a writer. Reflecting on your writing is like putting on a pair of glasses that allow you to see the areas where you need to sharpen your focus. It's like being a detective investigating your own work, uncovering patterns that you might have missed otherwise. Perhaps you've been relying too heavily on a certain word or phrase, like a security blanket you just can't seem to let go of. Or maybe your paragraphs are like disjointed puzzle pieces that need a little extra finesse to fit together seamlessly. Whatever the case may be, taking the time to reflect on your writing can help you identify these issues and take action to improve your overall writing skills.

Reflection also helps you with self-development. It's a chance to fine-tune your strengths and work on your weaknesses, helping you develop your own unique style. Think of your writing voice like a fingerprint - it's one-of-a-kind and uniquely yours. By reflecting on your writing, you can start to uncover what makes your writing sing and what might need a little more practice to hit those high notes. Perhaps you need to switch up your melody by adding more descriptive details or playing with the tempo of your sentences. Or maybe you need to adjust the pitch of your tone to better resonate with your intended audience. Regardless, reflection can help you develop your writing voice and create a sound that's all your own.

Reflection also helps you to pick up on some of your writing mistakes. For most writers, the process is the ultimate trial and error experiment. We've all been there, trying to fit a square peg in a round hole or cramming too many ideas into one sentence. We all make mistakes, but the key is to learn from them and use them as an opportunity to grow. Reflection allows you to take a step back and look at your work with a critical eye, identifying areas where you may have gone wrong and figuring out how to improve. For example, you may notice that you tend to write long, complicated sentences that are difficult to follow. By reflecting on your writing, you can start to simplify your writing and make it more accessible to your audience. Think of it as decluttering your writing closet - sometimes, less is more.

If you want to be a successful writer, it's crucial to treat reflection as a priority, not an afterthought. It's like scheduling a date with yourself - a time to slow down, take a deep breath, and get in touch with your inner writer. Just like you block off time for reading and writing, it's essential to schedule time specifically for reflection on your work.

You might choose to set aside a weekly "writing date" with yourself, where you review what you've written, assess your progress, and brainstorm new ideas. This could involve taking a critical eye to your work, looking for areas where you can improve, and developing an action plan to address those weaknesses.

Alternatively, you could make daily freewriting a part of your routine. Freewriting is like a warm-up exercise for your writing muscles, helping you tap into your thoughts and feelings about your work. You can use this time to write about your successes and challenges, your fears and doubts, or any other thoughts or emotions that come up for you. The goal is to tune into your writing mindset and get into a creative flow.

Regardless of how you choose to approach reflection, the key is to be intentional about it. Don't let it fall to the wayside or get buried under the weight of other demands. Make it a priority, and set aside the time you need to focus on it. Think of it as an investment in your growth as a writer - one that will pay dividends in the quality of your work. Make reflection a priority, and watch your writing skills soar.

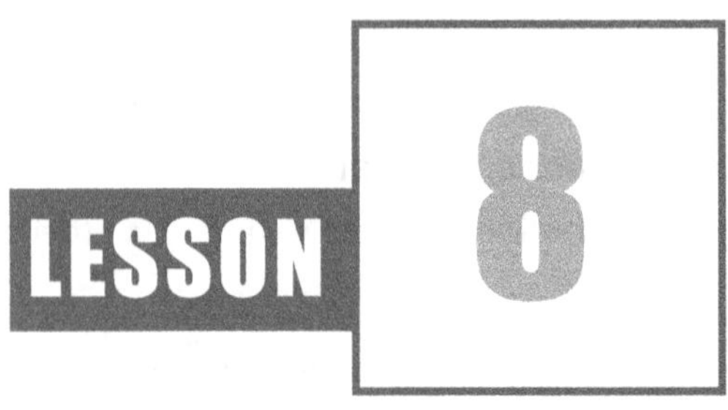

A Slice of the P.I.E.
(Persuade, Inform, Entertain)

It's important to remember that the world of literature is incredibly competitive. With so many talented writers vying for the attention of agents, producers, publishers, and readers, it can be easy to feel discouraged or overwhelmed. One way to stay ahead of the game is to always bring your creativity when it's time to work on a project. Whether you're crafting a compelling plot, developing dynamic characters, or writing beautiful prose, it's essential to think outside the box and find ways to stand out.

Creativity is the engine that drives innovation and progress. It is the force that turns dreams into reality, and ideas into action. Without creativity, our world would be a drab and lifeless place, devoid of beauty and innovation. Yet, too often, creativity is stifled and silenced by the pressures of everyday life. We are told to conform, to fit in, to follow the rules. We are told that creativity is a luxury, something to be indulged in only when all the "real work" is done.

But the truth is, creativity is not a luxury. It is a necessity. Without it, we are trapped in a world of monotony and sameness. We need creativity to bring color and vibrancy to our lives, to challenge us, and to inspire us to greatness. As the famous writer and artist, Austin Kleon once said, "Creativity is not a talent. It's a way of operating."

Indeed, creativity is not something that can be learned or taught. It is something that must be nurtured and cultivated, like a garden. It requires patience, perseverance, and a willingness to take risks and explore the unknown. The creative process is a messy one. It is full of false starts and dead ends, of frustration and doubt. But it is also full of moments of inspiration and breakthroughs, of joy and fulfillment. We must make time for creativity, for it is the fuel that drives our dreams and aspirations. We must give ourselves permission to explore and experiment, to make mistakes and learn from them.

We must not lose sight of our inner child, of the curiosity and wonder that fuels our creativity. We must embrace our quirks and idiosyncrasies, our passions and interests, and let them guide us on our creative journeys. Creativity is not just a way of operating. It is a way of living. It is the expression of our deepest selves, the manifestation of our dreams and aspirations. It is the spark that ignites our imaginations and the force that propels us forward.

Along with exploring your creativity, it's important to have a clear understanding of what you want your writing to accomplish. One useful framework for this is P.I.E., which stands for **P**ersuade, **I**nform, and **E**ntertain. Each of these elements represents a different goal that your writing can achieve. Persuasion involves convincing your audience to take a specific action or adopt a particular point of view. Informing involves conveying facts and data to your readers. Entertainment involves capturing your readers' interest and keeping them engaged with your writing. By keeping these three elements in mind, you can ensure that your writing is well-rounded and effective, and that it resonates with your intended audience.

Writing To Persuade

As writers, we have the power to move mountains with our words. We can inspire, enlighten, and entertain. One potent tool in our arsenal is the power of persuasion. We can convince our readers to take a particular action or adopt a specific point of view. We have the ability to change the world.

So, what is persuasion? At its core, it's the art of convincing others to see things from our perspective. It's the ability to build a case for our ideas, using logic, reason, and emotion to sway others to our side. Like any art, persuasion requires practice, skill, and a certain degree of finesse.

To be a persuasive writer, we must start with a clear understanding of our audience. We must know who they are, what they care about, and what motivates them. It's not enough to simply make an argument; we must make an argument that speaks directly to their needs and desires. We must understand their hopes, fears, and aspirations, and craft language that resonates with them on a deeper level.

One metaphor for persuasion is that of a dance. Just as a skilled dancer must be attuned to the movements of their partner, a persuasive writer must be attuned to the needs of their audience. They must lead them gracefully across the dance floor, guiding them with precision and grace. But they must also be flexible, ready to adapt to the movements of their partner at any moment. The dance of persuasion is a delicate one, but when executed correctly, it can be a thing of beauty.

Another key to effective persuasion is to build a strong case for our argument. This means presenting evidence, data, and examples that support our claims. It means anticipating and responding to counterarguments, and addressing any potential objections that our readers might have. It's comparable to being a lawyer in a courtroom. Just as a lawyer must present a compelling case to a judge and jury, a persuasive writer must present a compelling case to their readers. They must marshal their evidence, make their arguments, and cross-examine their opponents with skill and precision.

But persuasion is more than just building a case. It's also about emotional resonance. It's about tapping into the hopes, fears, and aspirations of our audience. This requires a strong sense of empathy and emotional intelligence, as well as the ability to craft language that is both vivid and evocative.

To become a better persuasive writer you must be clear and concise. When making an argument, it's essential to get to the point quickly and clearly. We must be able to distill our ideas down to their essence, and communicate them with clarity and precision. When looking to be persuasive you can tap into the art of storytelling. Stories have a powerful emotional resonance that can help to convey complex ideas in a way that is both relatable and memorable. By weaving stories into our arguments, you can make your ideas more compelling and resonant.

Also be sure to add humor. As a seasoned author, I can attest to the fact that incorporating humor into your writing can be an incredibly effective way to connect with your readers. However, using humor requires a great deal of skill, finesse, and a deep understanding of your audience. First and foremost, it's essential to ensure that your humor is appropriate for your readership. What's considered funny to one person may not be to another, so it's crucial to know your audience and what type of humor resonates with them.

Remember that humor should be used strategically, and not as a crutch to prop up weak content. If your writing isn't strong, no amount of humor can save it. When done well, humor can have a profound impact on your readers, making your content more memorable, relatable, and engaging. It can also help you to build a stronger connection with your readers, as they'll feel like they're getting to know the person behind the words. By mastering the art of persuasion, we can build a strong case for our ideas, connect with our readers on a deeper level, and move them to take action.

Writing To Inform

To effectively inform our readers, we need to present facts and data in a captivating manner that grabs their attention and leaves a lasting impression. This involves prioritizing clarity and engagement while ensuring that our message remains informative and meaningful. It's important to get straight to the point and express our ideas in a way that's easy to understand, especially when dealing with complex or technical information. By presenting our message with precision and artistry, we can create a narrative that both educates and entertains, providing our readers with a deeper understanding of the world.

One way to enhance clarity is to use visual aids, such as charts, graphs, and infographics. These tools can be used to help make complex data more accessible and understandable. A well-designed graph or chart can help clarify the message and make it more memorable. Readers are more likely to remember information that is presented in a visual format.

Another technique for conveying information is to use anecdotes and stories. A story can help create an emotional connection between the reader and the information being conveyed. This is important, as readers are more likely to remember information that resonates with them emotionally. A well-told story can also help illustrate a point in a way that is relatable.

Maya Angelou once said, "I've learned that people will forget what you said, people will forget what you did, but people will never forget how you made them feel." This quote speaks to the importance of emotional resonance when conveying information. When you can connect with your readers on an emotional level, you are more likely to create a lasting impact.

In addition to using anecdotes and stories, you can also use metaphors and analogies to convey complex ideas. A metaphor is a figure of speech that describes one thing in terms of another. By comparing one thing to another, you can create a mental picture that helps the reader understand the information being conveyed.

An analogy is a comparison between two things, which can help explain a complex concept in simpler terms. For example, imagine you are trying to explain the concept of climate change to a layperson. Instead of launching into a technical explanation of atmospheric carbon dioxide, you might use a metaphor to make the concept more relatable. You might say, "*Climate change is like a fever that our planet is experiencing. Just like a fever is a symptom of an underlying illness, climate change is a symptom of the underlying human activities that are causing the earth to heat up*." This metaphor helps make the concept of climate change more tangible and easier to understand.

Just like writing to persuade, adding humor to your work can also help with conveying information. When used appropriately, humor can make information more engaging and memorable. A well-placed joke or humorous anecdote can help lighten the mood and make the information more enjoyable to read. However, it is important to be careful when using humor, as it can easily backfire and detract from the message.

Conveying information is a complex task that requires skill and creativity. To be effective at conveying information you can use visual aids, weave stories and metaphors into your data and facts, and connect with your readers on an emotional level.. As writers, our mission is to educate, enlighten, and inspire our readers, and with the right tools and techniques, we can achieve that goal.

Writing To Entertain

There's no better feeling than having your readers on the edge of their seats, eagerly flipping through the pages of your work. Whether you're writing a suspenseful thriller, a romantic comedy, or an epic fantasy adventure, the key to success is capturing your readers' interest and emotions, and keeping them engaged with your skills. There are some tried-and-true techniques that you can use to create compelling, entertaining content that readers will love. One of the most important of these techniques is the use of relatable, well-developed characters.

Think about it: the reason we love characters like Harry Potter, Katniss Everdeen, Tony Montana, Bigger Thomas and Heidi Kachina is because they're complex, multi-dimensional, and relatable. We see a bit of ourselves in these characters, and that makes us care about what happens to them.

Another important technique for capturing readers' interest is through vivid and engaging descriptions. By painting a rich and detailed picture of the world and the characters you are creating, you can transport the reader to another place and time, immersing them in your story and capturing their imagination.

Of course, we have to be careful not to go overboard with our descriptions. We don't want to bore our readers to death with endless paragraphs about the color of the sky or the shape of a character's nose. The key is to strike a balance between detail and brevity. We want to give our readers enough information to make the world and the characters feel real, without overwhelming them with unnecessary details.

A great example of a writer who is able to transport readers to a different world is James Baldwin. In his novel 'Go Tell It on the Mountain,' Baldwin paints a vivid picture of life in Harlem during the 1930s. Through his masterful use of language, he captures the beauty and complexity of the community, its struggles and triumphs, and the human experience in general. Baldwin's immersive writing style draws the reader in, allowing them to experience the sights, sounds, and emotions of a different time and place.

Another effective technique for keeping readers engaged is through the use of plot twists and surprises. When readers are caught off guard by a sudden plot twist or surprise, they're more likely to be enthusiastically invested in the story and eager to find out what happens next.

However, you have to be careful not to rely too heavily on plot twists. You don't want to create a story that's so convoluted and confusing that your readers have no idea what's going on. As the great Mark Twain once said, "The difference between the almost right word and the right word is really a large matter—'tis the difference between the lightning bug and the lightning." In other words, you have to choose your plot twists and surprises carefully, making sure they fit organically into the story and don't feel forced or contrived.

Finally, pacing is essential for creating entertaining content. By carefully balancing action and exposition, and by using cliffhangers and other suspenseful techniques, you can create a story that's both engaging and emotionally impactful. Pacing refers to the speed and rhythm at which events in a story unfold. It is a critical aspect of storytelling because it determines how much time the author spends on each event, and how quickly the story moves forward. A well-paced story is one in which the events unfold at a speed that keeps the reader engaged, without moving so quickly that important plot points are missed. Overall, pacing is a critical element of storytelling, and can make the difference between a story that is engaging and entertaining, and one that falls flat.

Like a skilled bartender pouring the perfect cocktail, a savvy writer knows how to mix just the right amount of action, exposition, and suspense to keep their readers hooked. By stirring up a carefully crafted blend of these ingredients, you can serve up a story that's strong, satisfying, and packs an emotional punch. So, if you want to keep your readers thirsting for more, make sure to shake things up with some well-placed action, stir in some savory exposition, and garnish with a tantalizing cliffhanger.

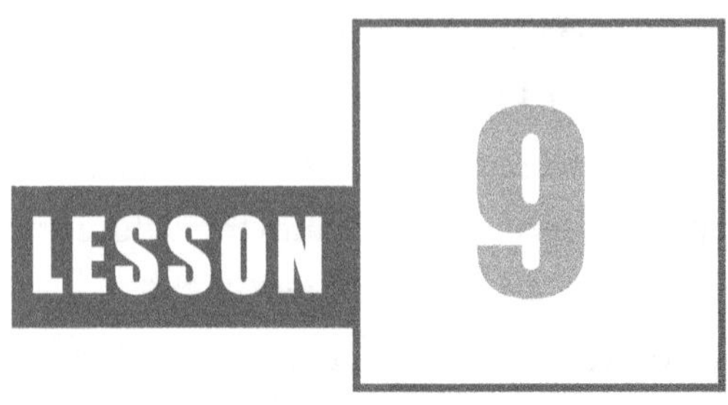

Write Smarter, Not Harder

> *If I had more time, I would have written a shorter letter."*
>
> \- Mark Twain

Writing is a creative process that involves tapping into one's own unique voice and style. When writing flows naturally, it can be a truly rewarding experience. It can feel like a deep and meaningful connection to one's own thoughts, emotions, and experiences, and can even help to unlock new levels of creativity and consciousness. This is why it is so important for writers to resist the urge to force their work or to follow formulas or templates that don't feel authentic to them.

Of course, this is not to say that writing is always easy or that it doesn't require skill or effort. Writing well takes practice and discipline, and it can be challenging to find the right words and structure for a piece of writing. When writers focus on the natural flow of their work and allow their ideas to come to them, rather than forcing them onto the page, the process can become much more enjoyable and rewarding.

In order to achieve this state of flow, writers must learn to trust their instincts and to let go of their inner critic. They must also be willing to experiment and take risks with their writing, rather than playing it safe. By doing so, they can tap into their own creativity and produce work that is truly unique and compelling. It would be inaccurate to say that writing is an easy task. However, there are a few strategies that you can use to streamline the creative process and make your life easier.

Plan Your Work

Writing is the perfect marriage of creativity and structure, of free-flowing inspiration and careful planning. And while the idea of planning your writing may seem at odds with the spontaneous nature of creativity, the truth is that a little bit of planning can go a long way in unlocking your full creative potential. The blank page can be a daunting foe, and the thought of wrestling with words and ideas for hours on end can be overwhelming. Planning your writing can be a great idea for overcoming these obstacles and unleashing your inner wordsmith.

Planning can take many different forms, from detailed outlines and chapter breakdowns to mind maps and brainstorming sessions. It's up to you to decide what works best for your unique writing style and project needs. But no matter what method you choose, the goal is always the same: to help you stay organized, focused, and inspired throughout the writing process. Planning can also be a fun and empowering experience! It's a chance to dream big, to play with ideas and concepts, and to explore new avenues of creativity. By taking the time to plan your writing, you're giving yourself the gift of clarity and direction, two things that are essential for any writer looking to create work that truly resonates with their audience.

Writing can be a long road. But as with any journey, it's important to have a guide. And that's where a writing journal comes in. A writing journal is a good tool that can help writers and authors of all levels stay organized, focused, and inspired throughout their creative journey. A writing journal can take many forms, from a simple notebook to a more elaborate system of digital files and folders. But the basic idea is the same: to create a space where you can capture your thoughts, ideas, and inspirations as they come to you.

Writing journals help you stay organized. By keeping all your notes and ideas in one place, you'll always know where to turn when you need a little inspiration or direction. But more than that, a writing journal is a way to connect with your innermost thoughts and emotions. It's a place to explore your fears and doubts, your hopes and dreams. It's a space to experiment with new ideas and to push the boundaries of your creativity.

A writing journal is also a great way to track your progress. It's a record of your journey, a reminder of how far you've come and how much you've accomplished. It's a source of motivation and inspiration on those days when the writing feels especially challenging. The most important thing is to keep writing. Whether you're capturing your thoughts in a journal, scribbling in the margins of a book, or typing away at your computer, the act of writing itself is what matters most.

Identify Your Audience

Your target audience is the group of people who are most likely to enjoy and appreciate your writing. Knowing your target audience is crucial if you want to create content that captivates, engages, and attracts new readers. One of the first steps to identifying your target audience is to define your genre and niche. *What type of writing do you fancy? What areas of expertise do you have? When you envision your readers, who do you envision?* Once you've found your niche, you can start picturing the type of people who would be spellbound by your work. For example, if you're into writing spine-chilling crime novels, your target audience would be people who can't get enough of thrillers and mysteries.

Conducting market research is a critical step in identifying your target audience, and it can be an enjoyable and exciting process that yields significant benefits for your writing. Market research allows you to gather data about your potential readers and understand their preferences, behaviors, and demographics. Using tools like Google Analytics, you can track the performance of your website and gain insights into your visitors' interests and behavior. For example, you can see which pages on your website are most popular, how long people are spending on your site, and where your traffic is coming from. This data can help you identify the types of content that are resonating with your audience, and adjust your writing strategy accordingly.

Social media platforms are another great source of data for market research. By analyzing your followers' interactions with your content, you can gain insights into their interests, preferences, and behavior. For example, you can see which posts get the most engagement, which hashtags are popular among your audience, and what type of content they are sharing. This information can help you tailor your writing to your target audience and create content that resonates with them.

Surveys are another powerful tool for conducting market research. You can use online survey tools to gather information about your readers' preferences, opinions, and behavior. For example, you can ask them what type of content they prefer, what topics they would like to see more of, and how often they read your writing. This information can help you create reader personas and tailor your writing to your target audience.

You can also create reader personas for your audience. A reader persona is an imaginary representation of your ideal reader, based on various demographics, interests, behaviors, and pain points. These personas can help you to develop a better understanding of your target audience and create content that resonates with them.

The process of creating reader personas involves conducting research to gather data about your potential readers. This data can come from a variety of sources, such as social platforms and even direct interactions with your existing readers. By collecting and analyzing this information, you can create detailed profiles of your ideal readers, including information such as their age, gender, occupation, interests, motivations, and challenges.

Once you have created your reader personas, you can use them as a guide for your writing. By understanding the needs and preferences of your target audience, you can create content that is relevant, engaging, and valuable to them. This can help you to attract new readers, retain existing ones, and build a loyal following. For example, if your reader personas indicate that your target audience is interested in health and fitness, you might write articles on topics such as healthy eating, exercise routines, or meditation. Or if your reader personas suggest that your audience is interested in personal finance, you might write articles on topics such as budgeting, saving for retirement, or investing.

Creating reader personas is an ongoing process. As you gain more data about your target audience, you may need to revise and update your personas to ensure that they accurately reflect your readers' preferences, interests, and behaviors.

An efficient strategy to pinpoint your audience is by identifying your reader's pain points. To capture the hearts and minds of your target audience, you need to get inside their heads and feel their pain. *What are their biggest challenges? What issues are they grappling with? What solutions are they desperately seeking?* By understanding the pain points of your readers, you can create content that provides practical solutions, answers, and insights that will have them coming back for more.

Getting to the heart of your readers' pain points involves a bit of detective work. You can engage with your readers directly through comments, emails, or social media to gain a more personal understanding of their needs. Once you have identified your readers' pain points, it's time to roll up your sleeves and get creative. Imagine you are a health and wellness blogger, and you've discovered that your readers are struggling with meal planning. You might create a blog post that provides meal planning tips, recipes, or hacks to make the process less daunting. By providing solutions to your readers' pain points, you can establish yourself as a trusted source of information and expertise in your niche.

Understanding your readers' pain points is also critical for developing products and services that resonate with them. If you are an author, for example, you might write a self-help book that provides guidance on overcoming common challenges related to your niche. Or if you are a content marketer, you might develop a course or coaching program that helps your readers tackle their pain points head-on.

Don't Rush The Process

Creating a work of art, such as a novel or screenplay, is no easy feat. It takes time, dedication, and a willingness to dive deep into the creative process. For many writers, the temptation to rush through the process and complete their project quickly can be strong. However, this often leads to subpar work that fails to capture the imagination of readers. Think of your writing like a garden. You can't simply plant a seed and expect it to immediately bloom into a beautiful flower. It takes time and patience to nurture that seed and help it grow into something beautiful. Writing is no different. Your ideas need time and attention to develop and grow into something truly special.

Rushing the creative process can cause unnecessary stress and anxiety, which can impact the quality of your work. Writing should be a process of discovery and exploration, where you have the freedom to experiment and make mistakes. Take your time to explore different avenues, and don't be afraid to go back and revise your work.

The beauty of writing is that there is no set timeline or deadline. While it's important to set goals and hold yourself accountable, it's equally important to embrace the creative process and allow yourself the time and space to create something truly extraordinary.

It's important to remember that the creative process is not a race, but rather a journey. Great writing requires patience, perseverance, and a willingness to dig deep and explore your innermost thoughts and emotions. Take your time, enjoy the journey, and trust that your hard work will pay off in the end. By embracing the creative process and allowing your ideas to flourish, you'll produce work that captures the imagination of readers and stands the test of time. Remember, writing is not about rushing to the finish line, but about the beauty of the journey.

No Participation Trophies

> *Participation trophies make you feel good when you are a kid, but in the real world, being just good enough for a participation trophy will get you fired!"*
>
> \- Unknown

Tommy was a young wordsmith with a natural talent for writing. His parents supported his passion for the written word and signed him up for writing competitions. Although Tommy never placed first, he was always handed a participation trophy for his efforts. He cherished those trophies and they became his prized possessions. As Tommy grew up, his love for writing continued to burn bright. However, he found himself unable to push himself beyond his comfort zone. He was content with receiving praise for his work, but lacked the competitive edge that is necessary to stand out in the writing world.

It wasn't until Tommy's mid-twenties that he realized the negative impact the participation trophies had on his motivation. He had grown complacent and had come to expect recognition and reward for simply participating, rather than striving for excellence. This realization was a bitter pill to swallow, but it also sparked a fire within him. Tommy was determined to break free from the complacency of his past. He knew that he needed to find the competitive spirit that had eluded him for so long. One day, while looking through his old possessions, he came across his childhood participation trophies. It was then that he realized how much those trophies had shaped his mindset. Tommy knew that he needed to work harder and challenge himself to become a better writer. He began entering writing competitions with the goal of winning, not just participating. The road was not easy, but he embraced the challenge with gusto.

Over time, Tommy's writing improved drastically. He began producing work that stood out and gained recognition in the writing world. His new competitive spirit had given him the drive and motivation he needed to excel.

Inside each of us, there is a "Tommy Mindset" that we must strive to overcome. Merely going through the motions and participating in a creative pursuit won't push us to achieve greatness. If we want to reach our full potential, we must aim to grow and evolve with our art. Each stroke of the pen or brush and every passing line of creation should fuel our motivation to become better and stronger. Let's push ourselves beyond the mediocre and unleash our true creative potential.

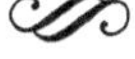

LESSON 10

BELIEVE IN YOURSELF

> "*Believe in yourself, take on your challenges, dig deep within yourself to conquer fears. Never let anyone bring you down. You got this.*"
>
> - Chantal Sutherland

Writing can be an intimidating and challenging task, and it can be easy to become discouraged or lose motivation. With the right mindset and self-care techniques, you can maintain a high level of vibration and self-assurance. One of the most important things for you to remember is that your work has value. Every writer has a unique perspective and voice, and your work can have a profound influence on the audience. It's important to remember this and to believe in yourself, even when the writing process is difficult or frustrating. In the face of rejection, criticism, or self-doubt, it is important for you to remain strong.

Stephen King is a prime example of a writer who had to push through rejection and self-doubt to achieve success. His first novel, Carrie, was rejected 30 times before it was finally published. But instead of giving up on his writing, King persisted. He kept submitting his work, even when it felt like he was hitting a brick wall. In interviews and in his memoir, King has spoken about the importance of persistence in his own writing career. He has said that "you can't be a writer if you don't write," and that it's essential to keep putting your work out there, even if it's not getting the response you want. King also emphasizes the importance of continuing to learn and improve as a writer, even after achieving success.

For King, persistence is not just about pushing through rejection and criticism, but also about putting in the time and effort to hone your craft. King is known for his prolific output, having written over 60 novels and 200 short stories in his career. This kind of output is only possible through a consistent and persistent writing practice.

Dealing With Self-Doubt

Self-doubt is a common experience for writers at all stages of their careers. Whether you're just starting out or you're a seasoned professional, it's easy to fall into a pattern of questioning your abilities and your worth as a writer. This can be a debilitating experience, as it can cause you to lose confidence in your work and ultimately give up on your writing goals. There are many factors that can contribute to self-doubt in writing. For example, if you've received negative feedback on your work or if you've experienced rejection from agents or publishers, or even your readers, it's easy to start questioning your abilities as a writer. Similarly, if you've been working on a project for a long time and you're not seeing the results you want, it can be easy to start feeling like you're not good enough or that your work isn't worth pursuing.

One of the most effective ways to combat self-doubt is to reframe your thinking around failure and rejection. Instead of seeing rejection as a sign of your own inadequacy, try to see it as a natural part of the writing process. Every successful writer has experienced rejection at some point in their career, and it's simply a sign that you need to keep working on your craft and improving your writing.

Think of rejection as a fork in the road. On one side of the fork, you have the option to give up on your writing dreams and pursue a different path. This road may seem easier or less painful in the short term, but it ultimately leads away from your ultimate goal of becoming a successful writer. On the other side of the fork, you have the option to persevere in the face of rejection and keep working on your craft. This road may be more challenging and require more effort and determination, but it ultimately leads to a more fulfilling career.

In this analogy, rejection is not a dead end, but rather a fork in the road that presents a choice. By choosing to view rejection as a natural part of the writing process, you can take the road that leads to success. It's important to remember that every successful writer has faced rejection and failure at some point in their career. Successful writers do not give up in the face of rejection, but instead they keep working on their craft and believing in their ability to succeed.

Ultimately, the key to overcoming self-doubt is to keep writing. As the saying goes, "the only way out is through." By continuing to work on your writing and staying committed to your goals, you can build your confidence and develop a sense of belief in yourself and your abilities. With time and practice, you can become a successful writer and achieve your dreams, despite any doubts or setbacks along the way.

No One Compares To You

The trap of comparison is one that many writers fall into, and it can be a major source of self-doubt and insecurity. It's natural to want to measure yourself against others, especially those who are more successful or accomplished than you. However, this kind of comparison can be incredibly damaging to your confidence and can make it difficult to believe in your own abilities. Imagine you're a runner who's just started training for a marathon. You're excited to start this new challenge and have set yourself a goal of running the race in under four hours. As you start to train, you begin comparing yourself to other runners who have already completed multiple marathons and can run at a much faster pace. You start to feel discouraged, like you'll never be able to achieve your goal, and you start to doubt your abilities as a runner.

It's important to remember that everyone's journey is different, and success is not a linear path. Comparing yourself to others can be damaging to your confidence and can hinder your progress. Instead of viewing other writers as competition, try to see them as mentors and sources of inspiration. Rather than focusing on what others have achieved, focus on your own progress and growth. Learn from their success and use it to motivate you to work harder and improve your own writing. Celebrate your successes, no matter how small they may seem. Set achievable goals for yourself and work towards them at your own pace. By focusing on your own journey and progress, you can avoid the negative impact of comparison and stay motivated to achieve your objectives.

Identifying your unique perspective is an important step in embracing your individuality as a writer. It's essential to understand what sets you apart from other writers, and to leverage your personal style. In your search for your uniqueness, take a good hard look at your life experiences and beliefs. Think of yourself as a cocktail, with each ingredient representing a different aspect of your identity. Shake it up, and you get a unique and flavorful concoction that only you can create.

Dealing With Outside Pressures

External pressures are a constant obstacle that can hinder your ability to create and produce written work. Financial and familial obligations, for example, can create a sense of guilt and shame for pursuing a career in writing. This can make it difficult for you to prioritize your craft and find the time and energy to work on your projects.

The financial pressures of the writing life can be particularly challenging. Many writers work multiple jobs in order to make ends meet, leaving little time for writing. This can create a sense of frustration and disappointment, as writers struggle to find the time and energy to pursue their passion. In order to get your projects done, some days you must make writing a priority. It's important to prioritize your craft, even if it means sacrificing other activities. This may require making tough choices, but carving out dedicated time for writing can be critical for staying motivated and productive. Be sure to set realistic financial goals. Create a budget that accounts for writing-related expenses, such as conferences, classes, or materials. This can help manage expectations and minimize financial stress. There are many resources available to writers, including grants, fellowships, and other funding opportunities. Take advantage of these resources when possible, and don't be afraid to ask for help or seek out advice from other writers or industry professionals.

In addition to financial obligations, familial responsibilities can make it difficult for writers to focus on their work. Parenting, caregiving, and other responsibilities can take up a significant amount of time and energy, leaving little room for creative pursuits. This can create a sense of guilt and frustration for writers, who may feel as though they are neglecting their writing in order to meet their familial obligations. For a lot of writers, it can be challenging to balance the demands of family life with the creative work of writing. However, it's essential to communicate with your family about your writing goals and needs.

One strategy you can deploy is the usage of boundaries. As a creative person, it is imperative that you set clear boundaries around your writing time. Let your loved ones know that you need that time to be uninterrupted, and ask for their support in creating a schedule that works for everyone. For example, if you're a parent, you might set aside an hour or two every evening after your children have gone to bed for writing. Let your partner know that during that time, you need to be left alone to focus on your work.

In addition to setting boundaries, it's also important to communicate your writing goals with your family members. Let them know why writing is important to you and what you hope to achieve through your work. This can help them understand why it's important to respect your writing time and support your creative endeavors.

Also remember that it's okay to ask for help when you need it. If you're feeling overwhelmed with your family obligations, don't be afraid to ask a partner, family member, or friend for assistance. Whether it's watching the kids for an afternoon or helping with household chores, having a support system can make it easier to find the time and energy to write. Communicating with your family about your writing goals and needs, setting clear boundaries around your writing time, and asking for help when you need it are all important steps to help you balance your family obligations with your creative pursuits. By working together with your loved ones, you can find a way to prioritize your writing while still meeting your familial obligations.

The Art of Self Care

As creative people, we have the ability to see the world in a unique way. We can create things that inspire, move, and bring joy to others. However, this gift comes at a cost. The creative process can be emotionally and mentally draining, leaving us feeling depleted and vulnerable. This is why it's so important to prioritize self-care as a creative person. Self-care isn't just about bubble baths and massages. It's about taking care of yourself physically, mentally, and emotionally so that you can continue to create and share your unique gifts with the world. As a creative person, you are responsible for your own well-being, and the more you prioritize self-care, the more you'll be able to thrive in your craft.

Let's start with physical self-care. Your body is your instrument, and it needs to be well-taken care of in order for you to be able to create your best work. This means making sure you're getting enough exercise, eating a healthy diet, and getting enough sleep. You don't need to become a gym rat or a health nut, but small changes like taking a walk each day or cutting back on junk food can make a big difference in how you feel.

Exercise is especially important for creative people because it helps to reduce stress. It can also boost your mood. When you're feeling stressed, anxious, or overwhelmed, taking a walk, practicing yoga, or going for a run can help you clear your head and feel more energized. Not only that, but exercise can also be a source of inspiration for your creative work. Many artists, writers, and musicians have found that physical movement helps to stimulate their creativity and bring forth new ideas.

Eating a healthy diet is also crucial for physical self-care. You need to nourish your body in order to have the energy and focus to create. This means choosing whole, nutrient-dense foods like fruits, vegetables, whole grains, and lean proteins. It's also important to drink plenty of water and avoid overloading your body with caffeine, sugar, and processed foods. Small changes like adding more greens to your meals or swapping out your afternoon soda for herbal tea can make a big difference in how you feel.

Getting enough sleep is essential for physical self-care. When you're well-rested, you have more energy, focus, and creativity. You need to protect your sleep time and create a bedtime routine that works for you. This might mean turning off screens an hour before bed, reading a book, taking a bath, or practicing relaxation techniques like meditation or deep breathing.

Now, let's move to mental self-care. The creative process can be emotionally challenging, and it's important to take care of your mental health in order to avoid burnout and stay inspired. There are many different ways to practice mental self-care, and it's important to find what works for you.

One tool for mental self-care is mindfulness. Mindfulness is the practice of being present in the moment and non-judgmentally observing your thoughts and feelings. When you're mindful, you're able to reduce stress, increase focus, and cultivate a sense of calm. There are many ways to practice mindfulness, such as meditation, deep breathing, or simply paying attention to your senses. You can also incorporate mindfulness into your creative process by taking breaks to observe nature, listen to music, or simply be present in the moment.

Therapy is another powerful tool for mental self-care. Most creators are more in touch with their emotions and vulnerabilities, and therapy can help them process these feelings and develop coping strategies. A therapist can also help you identify and address any underlying mental health issues that may be affecting your creative process. Therapy can also provide a safe space for you to talk about your fears, anxieties, and doubts, and help you find ways to move past them.

Finally, let's talk about emotional self-care. The creative process can be emotionally intense, and it's important to take care of your emotions in order to stay balanced and inspired. Emotional self-care means learning to recognize and express your feelings in healthy ways.

Unlocking the power of creative expression is a surefire way to boost your emotional wellbeing. Whether you're wielding a pen, paintbrush, or musical instrument, you can use the power of art to process your emotions and make sense of life's ups and downs. Don't let self-doubt hold you back – anyone can tap into their creativity for a little emotional self-care. Maybe writing your thoughts in a journal or capturing moments through photography will speak to you, or perhaps the freedom of dance will be your outlet of choice. Whatever form your creativity takes, it can be a powerful tool for cultivating a healthy relationship with your emotions.

An integral component of emotional self-care is creating a network of supportive relationships. As a creative individual, having people in your life who appreciate and understand your artistic expression is vital. This can take the form of a community of like-minded artists or a close friend or family member who you can rely on to offer encouragement and lend an ear when needed. It can feel daunting to reach out and establish connections with others, but building a supportive network requires vulnerability and the courage to take risks. By cultivating these relationships, you can gain a sense of belonging and validation, which can be essential for your emotional well-being as a creative person.

To sum up, self-care is an indispensable element for creative individuals who aspire to stay motivated, healthy, and harmonious. Physical self-care is essential for maintaining a healthy body, mental self-care is crucial for a sound mind, and emotional self-care is vital for a healthy heart. By prioritizing self-care, you will be better equipped to cope with the obstacles that come with the creative journey and to showcase your distinct talents to the world. Keep in mind that self-care is a continuous process rather than a destination, and it's crucial to treat yourself with kindness and compassion as you navigate the highs and lows of the creative life.

The Power of Positive Affirmations

Positive affirmations are a formidable ally for writers and authors, allowing them to boost their self-belief and trust in their abilities. These affirmations are constructive declarations that are repeated to oneself, serving to reframe and reshape one's thought processes and beliefs.

With sustained practice, affirmations can be instrumental in nurturing a positive mindset and enhancing one's self-assurance. By regularly reciting affirmations, writers and authors can build a sense of self-worth and encourage a productive and optimistic approach to their work.

For a writer or author, positive affirmations can be especially helpful in combating the common self-doubt that often accompanies the creative process. Many writers struggle with feelings of inadequacy or imposter syndrome, which can hold them back from realizing their full potential. However, by using affirmations to counteract these negative beliefs, writers can begin to shift their thinking and develop a more positive outlook on their abilities.

One way to use affirmations is to write them down and post them in a visible place, such as on your computer screen or in your writing space. This can help to keep your affirmations top of mind and remind you to use them throughout the day. Some examples of positive affirmations for writers and authors include:

- I am a talented writer with a unique voice.
- My writing is valuable and worthy of recognition.
- I trust my creative instincts and ideas.
- I am confident in my ability to tell a compelling story.
- My writing inspires and connects with others.

It's important to choose affirmations that feel authentic and resonate with you personally. When using affirmations, it's also helpful to focus on the present moment and to use language that is positive and empowering. For example, instead of saying "I will be a successful writer someday," you might say "I am a successful writer who is constantly growing and evolving."

Unlocking the potential of positive affirmations can be a game-changer for writers and authors looking to unleash their full creative power. By harnessing affirmations to counter negative self-talk and foster a positive mindset, writers can elevate their mental game and cultivate the confidence needed to truly excel in their craft. Be sure to select affirmations that strike a personal chord and blend them seamlessly with other self-care rituals. With dedication and commitment, you can nurture a steadfast belief in yourself and your writing, paving the way for limitless creative possibilities.

BONUS LESSON

START WHERE YOU ARE

"*Hold fast to dreams, for if dreams die, life is a broken-winged bird that cannot fly.*"

- Langston Hughes

Throughout the course of my writing career, which has spanned many decades, I have had the pleasure of traveling to many places and embarking on countless creative projects. I consider myself incredibly fortunate to have been blessed with the opportunity to encounter a multitude of faces and places that have shaped my perspective and enhanced my creativity. My journey as a writer began when I was just a child, clutching a humble #2 pencil as I conjured up my very first character. From that moment on, I knew that writing was my destined calling, the beacon that would guide me through the many years to come.

As any writer can attest, the writing bug can take years, even decades to discover. Some are born with an innate talent for wordplay, while others must tirelessly study and refine their craft to achieve their goals. Regardless of the path we take, the unrelenting passion and love for the written word is what drives us forward, encouraging us to explore new horizons and push the boundaries of what is possible in the realm of literature.

On my personal quest to discover innovative ways to bring the characters, settings, and plot twists that dance in my imagination to life, I've encountered countless aspiring authors and writers who seek the elusive recipe for crafting groundbreaking projects. Regardless of the setting, region, or nature of the interaction, most writers bombard me with the same question: "How do I get started?"

I always respond with the same answer: Start Where You Are!

From the dawn of humanity, many writers and authors have produced exceptional works of literature despite facing extreme adversity. Some have persevered through physical, emotional, societal, economic, and personal challenges to create enduring pieces of writing. Soldiers and military personnel have written on the battlefield, while incarcerated individuals have produced masterpieces within the confines of their cells. Some writers have even written their best works by candlelight and some by moonlight.

When it comes to starting a project, there is no one right way to begin. You can start in the middle, with no clear idea of where the project will ultimately lead, or even write the last sentence first and work backward. Creativity is infinite, with no set beginning or end. The most important thing is to start where you are, whether that be emotionally, physically, socially, or holistically. Ultimately, the key to success is to begin with what you have, no matter the circumstances.

It's Alive!

In the summer of 1816, Mary Shelley found herself living in a cramped and dimly lit rented room in Geneva, Switzerland. Her husband, the poet Percy Bysshe Shelley, and their infant son were with her, but their small abode was sparsely furnished, and their belongings few. The circumstances were grim, and the scandal surrounding their relationship had driven them from their native England.

Yet, despite her poverty and the weight of societal judgment, Mary's passion for writing burned bright. She was just eighteen years old when she began crafting her first book. The story poured forth from her pen in longhand, each word carefully chosen, every sentence a labor of love. The tale of a mad scientist who creates a monster and unleashes chaos on the world explored themes of mortality and the dangers of playing God. Mary drew from her own experiences of loss and grief, having lost her mother at a young age and experienced the pain of childbirth. Writing provided an escape from her impoverished reality, a portal into a world of her own creation. She worked tirelessly, pushing past her own doubts and the limitations imposed by her difficult circumstances. In doing so, she achieved a feat that would change literature forever.

Published in 1818, "Frankenstein" became an instant sensation, captivating readers with its chilling tale of horror and scientific ambition gone awry. The novel was a testament to Mary's courage and creativity, a triumph of the human spirit over adversity. Mary Shelley's legacy still endures today. It's testament to the power of imagination and the potential for greatness within us all, regardless of our circumstances. Her story reminds us that even in the darkest of times, we can find hope and inspiration if we are willing to reach beyond the limitations of our own minds and follow our passions with unwavering determination.

Mary Shelley's "Frankenstein" has had a significant cultural impact for over two centuries, inspiring numerous adaptations and products. From merchandise to graphic novels, the story has continued to captivate a wide range of fans, who have helped to carry on its legacy. Billions of dollars worth of merchandise have been sold over the years, a testament to the enduring popularity of the iconic scientist, monster and the young brave woman behind the story.

Legacy

Literature has the remarkable ability to transcend time, carrying with it the ideas and stories of its creators far beyond their lifetime. The legacy of writers can inspire future generations to continue the tradition of storytelling, passing on the torch of creativity from one generation to the next. The impact of the written word is profound, and it's humbling to think that the stories we write can touch the lives of people we may never meet, bringing us together in a shared human experience.

The ability of books and literature to outlive their creators is a form of immortality. It allows their legacy to continue, long after they have passed away. The words that we love can become a source of comfort and inspiration, providing a window into the minds and hearts of the writers who came before us. When we read their work, we are connected to their thoughts and ideas, and we are transported into their world.

To all the writers, authors, creators, playwrights, and content creators out there, the power to create is in your hands. The creative process can be intimidating, but it is essential to start where you are and take that first step towards your goals. Remember that there is no one right path to success, and each writer must find their unique route. Take any step forward, no matter how small it may be. Every step counts, and progress is progress, no matter how small.

As writers, we must embrace the power of creation and stay motivated to make progress towards our dreams. It's essential to surround ourselves with supportive people who can offer guidance and encouragement. We must also be our own cheerleaders, reminding ourselves of our strengths and believing in our abilities to achieve our goals. Embrace the power of creation and never give up. Best of luck and happy writing!

ABOUT THE AUTHOR

★★★

Dashawn Taylor is a bestselling author and highly sought-after ghostwriter, whose projects have appeared on some of the most prominent platforms, including HBO, MTV, BET, NBC, VH1, The New York Times, and Essence Magazine. With an impressive career spanning over two decades, Dashawn has collaborated with Grammy Award-winning artists, world leaders, Super Bowl champions, and dozens of professionals in various fields.

Dashawn is a graduate of Rutgers University, where he honed his writing skills and developed a deep passion for storytelling. Since releasing his first book "*From Poverty to Power Moves*", Dashawn has authored, ghostwritten, and provided literary services for over 100 projects, many of which have become instant bestsellers. His love for the art has driven him to inspire creators with his W.I.N. (Writing Is Necessary) initiative that aims to help writers elevate their talent to the next level.

WORDPLAY

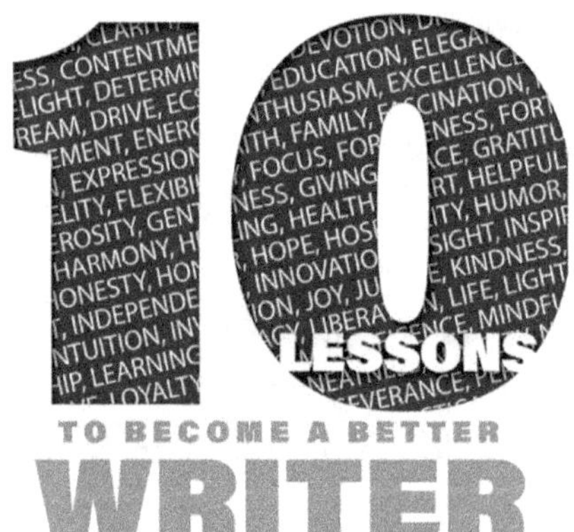

TO BECOME A BETTER

WRITER

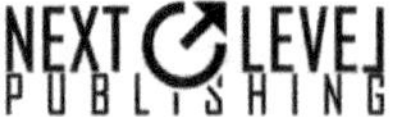

WWW.NEXTLEVELPUBLISHING.COM
WWW.DASHAWNTAYLOR.COM

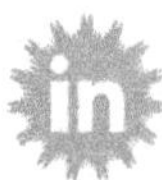
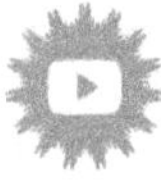
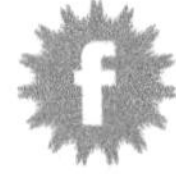
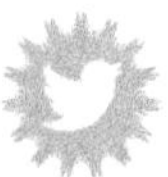
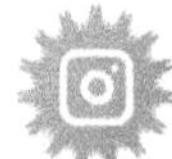

@DASHAWNTAYLOR

www.ingramcontent.com/pod-product-compliance
Lightning Source LLC
LaVergne TN
LVHW020633100826
845148LV00012B/2173